Twilight of Empire

Twilight of Empire

Two Accounts of
Napoleon's Journeys in Exile
to Elba and St. Helena

Narrative of Events
by Sir Thomas Ussher

Napoleon's Last Voyage
Extract From a Diary by
Sir George Cockburn

*Twilight of Empire: Two accounts of Napoleon's
Journeys in Exile to Elba and St. Helena
Narrative of Events* by Sir Thomas Ussher
Napoleon's Last Voyage Extract of a diary by Sir George Cockburn

First published under the titles
A Narrative of Events &c.,&c. 1841
and
Napoleon's Last Voyage 1888

Leonaur is an imprint of Oakpast Ltd

Copyright in this form © 2009 Oakpast Ltd

ISBN: 978-1-84677-648-9 (hardcover)
ISBN: 978-1-84677-647-2 (softcover)

http://www.leonaur.com

Publisher's Notes

In the interests of authenticity, the spellings, grammar and place names used have been retained from the original editions.

The opinions of the authors represent a view of events in which he was a participant related from his own perspective, as such the text is relevant as an historical document.

The views expressed in this book are not necessarily those of the publisher.

Contents

Narrative of Events   7
Napoleon's Last Voyage   77

Narrative of Events

by Thomas Ussher

Contents

Journal of Events   10
Appendix   49
Copie Des Articles Du Traité De Paris   58
From Elba To Paris,   63

Journal of Events, Connected With the Emperor Napoleon

In the month of August, 1813, I was stationed in the *Undaunted* frigate, in the Gulf of Lyons, with the *Redwing*, Sir John Sinclair, and the *Espoir*, the Hon. Captain Spencer, under my orders. The latter, who had joined sometime before, had brought me letters and papers from England, in which were various reports of the reverses of the French army, and of the probable downfall of the Emperor Napoleon, with many speculations and surmises thereupon, and hinting at the possibility of his attempting to make his escape to America. The *Courier* newspaper even went so far as to insert in its columns a minute description of the Emperor's person, in case the attempt should be made. Singularly enough, I cut out the paragraph in question, and wafered it on the bookcase in my cabin, jokingly observing to the other captains, who happened to be dining with me about that time, that they had better take a copy of it, as he might possibly come our way, little imagining at the time I made this observation, that a few short months would see him at the very same table at which we were then sitting.

The *Redwing* and *Espoir* afterwards returned to England, and I remained through the winter cruising off the coast of France. On the 24th of April, 1814, about ten o'clock at night, being five or six leagues from the town of Marseilles, in company with the *Euryalus*, Captain Charles Napier, then under my orders, my attention was attracted by a brilliant light, in the direction of, and seemingly coming from the town, which I conjectured was an illumination for some important event. I began to think the *Courier* might prove, after all, to be a true prophet. Every exertion was then made, and every sail set in both ships to work up the bay. At daybreak we were close off the land all was apparently quiet in the batteries, not a flag flying, nor were the telegraphs, which was uniformly the case on the approach of an enemy, at work. Everything betokened that some great change had taken place.

The morning was serene and beautiful, with a light wind from the southward. Eager to know what had happened, but above all, anxious to hear (for who that has once experienced the horrors and miseries of war, can wish for its continuance!) that peace had been restored, I pushed in towards the island of Pomegue, which protects the anchorage of the bay of Marseilles. To guard against a surprise, however, should such be attempted, I took the precaution of clearing the ship for action, and made signal to the *Euryalus* to shorten sail, that in the event of the batteries opening unexpectedly upon the *Undaunted*, my friend, Captain Napier, by whose judgment and gallant conduct I had on former occasions profited, might render me any assistance, in the event of being disabled.

We now showed our colours and hoisted a flag of truce, and the royal standard of the Bourbons, which the ship's tailor had made during the night, at the main. This flag had not been displayed on the French coast for a quarter of a century: thus equipped, we were allowed to approach within gunshot, when we observed men coming into the battery, and almost immediately a shot struck us on the main deck. Finding it was not their intention to allow us to proceed, I ordered the ship to be wore round, and hauled down the flag of truce and standard. While wearing, a second shot was fired, which dropped under the counter.

This unusual and unwarrantable departure from the rules of civilised warfare, I resolved to notice, in the only way such attacks ought to be noticed, determined at once, in the promptest and most energetic way, to convince our assailants, that under no circumstances was the British flag to be insulted with impunity. I, therefore, again wore round, and arriving within point blank shot of the battery, poured in a broadside, which swept it completely, and in five minutes not a man was to be seen near the guns. It was entirely abandoned. I now made sail for a second battery, and by signal directed the *Euryalus* to close, intending to anchor off the town. Shortly afterwards, observing a boat with a flag of truce, standing out of the harbour, I shortened sail to receive it.

On coming alongside, I found she had on board the mayor and municipal officers of Marseilles, who had come from the town to apologise for the conduct pursued by the batteries, and intimating that it was an unauthorised act of some of the men. They informed me of the abdication of Napoleon, and the formation of a provisional government at Paris; and I congratulated them on the change. I assured these gentlemen, that with regard to the conduct of the batteries, I could have no hesitation in forgiving all that had passed, and that I only hoped might be as easily forgiven for the part I had taken; that to prove my confidence in the honour and loyalty of their city, I should anchor my ship abreast of the town, a proposition they did not seem very much to approve of. I then made sail, with the *Euryalus* in company, and dropt anchor in the mouth of the harbour, that I might be the better able to take advantage of any circumstances that might occur. Captain Napier and myself then proceeded in the barge of the *Euryalus* towards the land. We found a dense crowd collected at the landing place, who, as we stopped to inquire for the Pratique officers, rushed into the water, and seizing the bow hauled her by main force on shore.

Never did I witness such a scene as now presented itself, as almost choked by the embraces of old and young, we were hoisted on their shoulders and hurried along, we knew not whither. I certainly did not envy the situation of my friend, Captain Napier, whom I saw most lovingly embraced, by an old lady with one eye, from whom he endeavoured, in vain, to extricate himself, not using, I must say, the most gentle terms our language affords. In this way we arrived at the Hotel de Ville, amidst loud cries of "*Vive les Anglais.*" We were here received by our friends, who had come with the flag of truce in the morning, but who were evidently not prepared for such a visit from us now. Indeed, under any other circumstances, we should not have been justified in appearing there as we did. Conscious, however, that we had no infectious disease on board, and as we had not visited any part of the Mediterranean where the plague prevails, we endeavoured to quiet their fears, and to satisfy them that no danger was to be apprehended from our visit. This infringement, however, of their sanitary laws (the observance of which they consider so essential to their safety,) they appeared to feel deeply, though I gave them every assurance of the healthy state of the ships. Besides, as I observed, it was no act of ours, but had been forced upon us by themselves, and under circumstances which we could not very well control. They said there was no previous instance of their sanitary laws having been violated, except by Napoleon, when he landed from Egypt.

They then invited us, with true French politeness, into the Maison de Ville, remarking, at the same time, how much their city had suffered in the reign of Louis XIV. from the dreadful plague, a magnificent picture of which, by David, showing some of the horrors of that visitation, hung in one of the principal rooms of the building. They now politely requested us to wait upon the general in command. We found that officer attending High Mass at the cathedral, and it is hardly possible to describe his astonishment, and the excitement caused by seeing two British naval officers, in their uniforms, in the midst of the congregation. I went up to the general, who received me with great apparent cordiality, and with considerable tact, (for we were at that time the greater "Lion" of the two,) invited us to join the procession, (I think it was that of the Virgin,) for which preparations had been made, and which was about to set out from the church where we then were. The streets through which we passed were excessively crowded, so much so, that it was with the utmost difficulty the procession could make its way at all. The predominance of old people and children among the crowd was remarkable. Observing upon this to some of the municipal officers, they told me that this was caused by the conscription, which had swept off, without distinction, (like another plague) all the young men who were capable of bearing arms, causing indescribable misery not only here, but everywhere throughout France. Happy, indeed, were these poor people at seeing us amongst them, the harbingers of peace, which many of them had so long and ardently desired. That this was the prevailing feeling among them their whole demeanour amply testified, as with vociferations, loud and vehement, of "*Vive les Anglais!*" they plainly told us we were not unwelcome visitors.

On arriving near the general's house, we were invited to take some refreshment, which we did; but the populace outside were very impatient, and were not satisfied till we again made our appearance amongst them. I now began to reflect on the singular and difficult circumstances in which I was placed, and the responsibility I was incurring, being positively without any information on which I could rely, as to the state of affairs outside of Marseilles.

Nevertheless, as I knew the ships were prepared for any emergency that might happen and in the hands of Lieutenant Hastings, my first lieutenant, in whose zeal and gallantry I had the greatest possible confidence; I did not think there was much cause for apprehension, come what might. I had an idea, indeed, that this enthusiasm would not last. In the midst of all this rejoicing, I received a communication from the Commandant of the town, informing me that he had been instructed by his superior the Prince of Esling, the Governor of Toulon, and commander-in-chief of the district, to order us to our ships, and to allow of no further communication, excepting by flags of truce. I replied to this somewhat insolent mandate, by declaring my determination to remain where I was, telling the Commandant pretty plainly that I should not comply with the prince's orders. I knew my strength, and that the ships, by their position, had the entire command of the town.

The prince then intimated that he would march three thousand men against the town. This also I was prepared for. During this angry discussion, Colonel Campbell, the English commissioner, arrived, bringing with him a very important note, which will be found in the appendix. I immediately waited upon him. He informed me that he had left the Emperor Napoleon on the road, pursuing his journey to St. Tropez, from which place, it had been arranged, he was to embark, accompanied by the envoys of the Allied Sovereigns. I immediately made arrangements for quitting the harbour of Marseilles, and on the following morning (April 26th) set sail for St. Tropez, leaving Captain Napier in command of the station.

Undaunted, off St. Tropez,
April 27th.

On arriving off St. Tropez, we hoisted a red flag at the main, being the distinguishing signal agreed upon with Colonel Campbell at Marseilles. A boat immediately came out of the harbour, with a lieutenant from the French frigate, *Dryade*, (commanded by the Comte de Montcabri,) which was lying there with the *Victorieuse* corvette. The Comte sent his lieutenant to inform me, that the Emperor Napoleon had abdicated, and that the Comte de Montcabri had orders from the Provisional Government to remain at St. Tropez, with the *Victorieuse*, for the purpose of conducting the Emperor to the island of Elba, the sovereignty of which island had been guaranteed to him by the Allied Sovereigns, (it now struck me, that the red flag at the main was considered, in war, a signal of defiance.) At this moment a boat came alongside, with an Austrian officer, Major Sinclair, dispatched from Frejus by Colonel Campbell, to inform me that at the particular request of the Emperor, the Commissioners of the Allied Sovereigns had thought proper to change the place of embarkation, and requesting me to proceed to Frejus Bay. Frejus is an open roadstead, five or six leagues to the north of St. Tropez.

Here it was that Napoleon landed on his return from Egypt, On arriving at the anchorage, I received a note from Colonel Campbell, informing me that horses had been sent down from the town, and an orderly sergeant placed at my disposal, to carry on any communications with the town. Frejus lies on a height, three or four miles from the anchorage. I took advantage of this conveyance and immediately waited on Colonel Campbell, who, although suffering severely from his wounds, immediately accompanied me to the Chapeau Rouge, a small *auberge* or hotel (and I believe the only one in Frejus,) where Napoleon was lodged, and whatever my previous feelings might have been towards this, the most powerful and constant enemy the country ever had to contend with, I am proud to confess, all resentment and uncharitable feeling, if any ever existed, quickly vanished, and I felt all the delicacy of the situation, in which circumstances the most extraordinary had placed me.

His faithful follower in adversity, Comte Bertrand, was in attendance, and having announced Colonel Campbell and myself, we were immediately presented to him. Napoleon was dressed in the regimentals of the "*Vielle Garde,*" and wore the star of the Legion of Honour; he walked forward to meet us, with a book open in his hand, to which he occasionally referred, when asking me questions about Elba, and the voyage thither, he received us with great condescension and politeness; his manner was dignified, but he appeared to feel his fallen state. Having asked me several questions regarding my ship, he invited us to dine with him, upon which we retired. I was shortly afterwards waited upon by Comte Bertrand, who presented me with lists of the baggage, carriages, horses, &c., belonging to the Emperor.

I immediately made arrangements for receiving them, and then demanded an interview with the several envoys of the Allied Sovereigns, feeling, that placed in a position of such peculiar responsibility and delicacy, it was necessary for me to learn from them the instructions they had received from their respective sovereigns, that I might shape my conduct accordingly, and particularly to know from them what ceremony was to be observed on Napoleon's embarkation, and on arriving on board the *Undaunted*, as I was desirous to treat him with that generosity towards a fallen enemy which is ever congenial to the spirit and feelings of Englishmen. They informed me that their instructions were precise and positive, and that he was styled by the treaty of Fontainbleau, Emperor and Sovereign of the island of Elba. I still entertained doubts as to the propriety of receiving him with a royal salute, but Colonel Campbell (in order to remove every doubt on that subject,) showed me Lord Castlereagh's instructions to him, which were conclusive. I now gave orders to embark the Emperor's baggage, carriages and horses.

Soon after, the *Dryade*, French frigate, and the *Victorieuse* corvette, arrived in the roads and anchored. The Comte de Montcabri, on landing, expressed his surprise to my first lieutenant, on seeing the baggage going on board. But on being presented to the Emperor shortly after, and learning his intention of embarking on board the *Undaunted* he returned to his ship and sailed out of the bay, with the *Victorieuse* in company. The *Victorieuse*, I was given to understand, was to have remained at Elba in the Emperor's service. The party at table consisted of the Prince Schouwallof, Russian envoy; Baron Roller, Austrian envoy; Comte Truxos, Prussian envoy; and our envoy, Colonel Campbell; Comte Clam, *aide-de-camp* to Prince Swartzenburgh; Comte Bertrand, Druo, and myself.

The Emperor did not appear at all reserved, but on the contrary, entered freely into conversation, and kept it up with great animation; he appeared to show marked attention to Baron Koller, who sat on his right hand. Talking of his intentions of building a large fleet, he alluded to the Dutch navy, of which he had formed a very mean opinion; he said that he had improved their navy, by sending able naval architects to Holland, and that he had built some fine ships there; the *Austerlitz* (he said) was one of the finest ships in the world; in speaking of her, he addressed himself to Prince Schouwallof, who did not seem to like the allusion; he said the only use he could make of the old Dutch men-of-war, was to fit them to carry horses to Ireland.

He talked of the Elbe, said the importance of that river was but little known, that the finest timber for ship building could be brought there, at a small expense, from Poland, &c. &c.

I slept this night at Frejus, and was awoke at four in the morning by two of the principal inhabitants, who came into my room, to implore me to embark the Emperor as quickly as possible, intelligence having been received that the army of Italy, lately under the command of Eugene Beauharnais, was broken up, that the soldiers were entering France in large bodies, and were as devoted as ever to their chief; these gentlemen were afraid the Emperor might put himself at their head, I informed them I had no more to do with embarking the Emperor than they had, and requested them to make known to the envoys (who, I dare say, were as little pleased as I was, in being awoke at so unseasonable an hour,) their fears and misgivings. It was, indeed, pretty evident that Napoleon was in no hurry to quit the shores of France, and appeared to have some motive for remaining.

The envoys became rather uneasy, and requested me to endeavour to prevail upon him to embark that day. In order to meet their wishes I demanded an interview, and pointed out to the Emperor the uncertainty of winds, and the difficulty I should have in landing in the boats, should the wind change to the southward and drive in a swell upon the beach, which, from the present appearance of the weather, would, in all probability, happen before many hours, in which case I should be obliged, for the safety of his Majesty's ship, to put to sea again; I then took leave and went on board, and at 10 o'clock received the following note from Colonel Campbell:

> Dear Ussher,
> The Emperor is not very well. He wishes to delay embarking for a few hours, if you think it will he possible then; that you may not be kept in suspense, he begs you will leave one of your officers here, who can make a signal to your ship when it is necessary to prepare, and he will also send previous warning. I think you had better come up, or send, and we can fix a signal, such as a white sheet

at the end of the street. The bearer has orders to place at your disposal a hussar and a horse, whenever you wish to go up or down, let me know your wishes by bearer. You will find me at General Roller's.
Yours truly,
N. Campbell
10, a.m.

Napoleon finding that it was my determination to put to sea saw the necessity of yielding to circumstances; Bertrand was accordingly directed to have the carriages ready at seven o'clock. I waited on the Emperor (at a quarter before seven) to inform him that my barge was at the beach; I remained alone with him in his room at the town, until the carriage, which was to convey him to the boat, was announced. He walked up and down the room, apparently in deep thought. There now was a loud noise in the street, upon which I remarked, that a French mob was the worst of all mobs; (I hardly know why I made this remark,) he replied, yes, they are a fickle people, and added, they are like a weathercock.

At this moment Comte Bertrand announced the carriages; he immediately put on his sword, which was lying on the table, and said, "*allons, capitaine*;"

I turned from him to feel if my sword was loose in the scabbard, fancying I might have occasion to use it. The folding doors (which opened on a pretty large landing place) were now thrown open, when there appeared a number of most respectable looking people, the ladies, in full dress, waiting to see him. They were perfectly silent; but bowed most respectfully to the Emperor, who went up to a very pretty young woman in the midst of the group, and asked her, in a courteous tone, if she was married, and how many children she had. He scarcely waited for a reply; but bowing to each individual, as he descended the staircase, stepped into his carriage, desiring Baron Koller, myself, and Comte Bertrand, (the Mareschal du Palais) to accompany him.

The carriage immediately drove off at full speed to the beach, followed by the carriages of the envoys. On arriving there the scene was deeply interesting. It was a bright moonlight night, with little wind; a regiment of cavalry was drawn up in a line upon the beach; and among the trees. On the carriage approaching, the bugles sounded, which, with the neighing of horses, and the noise of the people assembled to bid *adieu* to their fallen chief, was to me in the highest degree interesting. The Emperor having left the carriage, embraced Prince Schouwallof, (who, with Comte Truxos, took leave and returned to Paris,) and, taking my arm, proceeded immediately towards the barge, which was waiting to receive us. Lieutenant Smith, (nephew of Sir Sidney Smith, who, it is well known, had been some time confined in the Temple with Captain Wright) was by a strange coincidence the officer in command of the boat. He came forward and assisted the Emperor along the gang-board into the boat. The *Undaunted* lay close in, with her topsails hoisted, lying to.

On arriving alongside, I immediately went up the side to receive the Emperor on the quarter-deck. He took his hat off and bowed to the officers who were all assembled on the deck. He soon afterwards went forward to the forecastle amongst the people, and I found him there conversing with those among them who understood a little French. Nothing seemed to escape his observation. The first thing which attracted his notice was the number of boats (I think we had eleven) Having made all sail, and fired a royal salute, I accompanied him to my cabin and shewed him my cot, which I had ordered to be prepared for him: he smiled when I said I had no better accommodation, and said that everything was very comfortable, and he was sure he would sleep soundly.

We now made all sail out of the bay, and shaped our course for Elba. At four, his usual hour, he was up, and had a strong cup of coffee, (his constant custom) and at seven came on deck, and seemed not the least affected by the motion of the ship; at this moment we were exchanging numbers with the *Malta*, (Sir Benjamin Hallowel, standing towards Genoa) and I telegraphed to him that I had the Emperor Napoleon on board. The wind having changed to the south-east, I hauled on the larboard tack towards Corsica, at ten we breakfasted; Comte Bertrand, Comte Druo, Baron Roller, Colonel Campbell, Comte Clam, and the officer of the morning watch were present. Napoleon was in good spirits, and seemed very desirous of showing that though he had ambition, England was not without her share also. He said, that ever since the time of Cromwell, we had set up extraordinary pretensions, and arrogated to ourselves the dominion of the sea that after the peace of Amiens, Lord Sidmouth wished to renew the former treaty of commerce, which had been made by Vergennes after the American war; but that he, anxious to encourage the industry of France, had expressed his readiness to enter into a treaty, not like the former, which it was clear, from the portfolio of Versailles, must be injurious to the interests of France; but on terms of perfect reciprocity, *viz.*, that if France took so many millions of English produce, England should take back as many millions of French produce in return. Lord Sidmouth said, "this is totally new; I cannot make a treaty on these conditions."

Very well! I cannot force you into a treaty of commerce no more than you can force me, and we must remain as we are without commercial intercourse. Then, said Lord Sidmouth, there will be war, for unless the people of England have the advantage of commerce secured to them, which they have been accustomed to, they will force me to declare war. As you please, it is my duty to study the just interests of France, and I shall not enter into any treaty of commerce on other principles than those I have stated that although England made *Malta* the pretext, all the world knew that was not the real cause of the rupture; that he was sincere in his desire for peace, as a proof of which, he sent his expedition to San Domingo.

When it was remarked by Colonel Campbell that England did not think him sincere, from his refusing a treaty of commerce and sending consuls to Ireland, with engineers, to examine the harbours; he laughed, and said, that was not necessary, for every harbour in England and Ireland was well known to him; and Bertrand remarked, that every ambassador was a spy.

Napoleon said that the Americans acknowledged the justness of his principles of commerce, formerly they brought over some millions of tobacco and cotton, took specie in return, and then went empty to England, where they furnished themselves with British manufactures. He refused to admit their tobacco and cotton unless they took from France an equivalent in French produce, they yielded to his system as being just; he added, that now England had it all her own way, that there was no power which could successfully oppose her system, and that she might now impose on France any treaty she pleased—

"*Les Bourbons pauvres diables* (here he checked himself,) *ils sont de Grands Seigneurs qui se contentent d'avoir leurs terres et leur chateaux, mais si le peuple Français devient me content de cela, et trouve qu'il n'y a pas l'encouragement pour leurs manufactures dans l'Interieur qu'ils devroit en avoir, ils seront chassés dans six mois. Marseilles, Nantes, Bordeaux, et la Côte ne se soucient pas de cela, car ils ont toujours le même commerce, mais dans l'interieur c'est autre chose. Je sais bien comment l'esprit etoit pour moi a Terrare, Lyons, et ces endroits qui des manufactures, et qui j'ai encouragés.*"

He said that Spain was the natural friend of France, and enemy of Great Britain, that it was the interests of Spain to unite with France in support of their commerce and foreign possessions—that it was a disgrace to Spain to allow us to hold Gibraltar, it was only to bombard it night and day for a year and it must eventually fall. He asked whether we still held Ceuta; he did not invade Spain, he said, to put one of his own family on the throne, but to revolutionize her, to make her a kingdom *en regle*, to abolish the inquisition, feudal rights, and the inordinate privileges of certain classes, he spoke also of our attacking Spain, without a declaration of war and without cause, and seizing the frigates bringing home treasure.

Someone remarked, that we knew Spain intended to make common cause with him as soon as the treasure should arrive; he said he did not want it, all he had was five millions (*francs*) per month. On my asking a question regarding the Walchern expedition, he said we could not hold Walchern with less than

14,000 men, half of whom would be lost annually by disease, and as he had such means in the neighbourhood at Antwerp, it could, at any time, be attacked, and by means of superiority of numbers must fall, that the expedition against it was on too great a scale and too long preparing, as it gave him time. He added that he wrote from Vienna, that the expedition was going to Antwerp. He thought a *coup-de-main* with ten thousand men, and with less preparation, would have succeeded laughed at our ignorance in suffering so much time to be lost, and sitting down before Flushing (whereby we lost a large proportion of our army through disease) instead of advancing rapidly on Antwerp, and seemed astonished at our government selecting such a commander-in-chief for so important an expedition.

After breakfast Napoleon read for some hours, and came on deck about two o'clock, and remained two or three hours, occasionally remarking what was going forward, as the men were employed in the ordinary duty of the ship, mending sails, drawing yarns, exercising the guns, &c. &c. After dinner he referred to a map of Toulon harbour, and went over the whole of the operations against Lord Hood and General O'Hara (he commanded the artillery there as major) all the other officers, he said, were for a regular siege; he gave in a memoir proposing to drive off the fleet from the inner harbour, which, if successful, would place the garrison of Toulon in danger that it was upon this occasion he felt the superiority of the new tactics. He related an anecdote of one of the representatives of the people, ordering his battery to fire and unmasking it too soon.

This evening a small Genoese trading vessel passed near us, I ordered her to be examined, and as Napoleon was anxious to know the news, I desired the captain to be sent on board; Napoleon was on the quarter-deck, he had a great-coat and round hat on. As he expressed a wish to question the captain, I sent him to him on the after part of the quarter-deck, and afterwards ordered him down to my cabin. "Your captain," said he, "is the most extraordinary man I ever met with, he put all sorts of questions to me, and without giving me time to reply, repeated the same questions rapidly to me a second time."

When I told him whom he had been speaking to he appeared all astonishment, and instantly ran on deck hoping to again see him; but Napoleon, to his great disappointment, had already left the deck and gone below. When I told Napoleon that the man had remarked the rapidity with which he put questions to him twice over, he said it was the only way to get at the truth from such fellows. One morning, when Napoleon was on deck, I ordered the ship to be tacked, and we stood towards the Ligurian coast; the weather was very clear as we approached the land; we had a fine view of the Alps; he leaned on my arm, and gazed at them with great earnestness for nearly half an hour; his eye appeared quite fixed. I remarked that he had passed those mountains on a former occasion, under very different circumstances; he merely said it was very true.

The wind was now increasing to a gale, he asked me, laughing, if there was any danger, which was evidently meant to annoy Baron Koller, who was near him, and who had no great faith in the safety of ships, and whom he constantly joked on his bad sailorship, as he suffered dreadfully from sea sickness. He made some observations to me as to our men's allowance of provisions, and seemed surprised that they had cocoa and sugar, and asked how long they had had that indulgence, I told him they were indebted to him for it, that the continental system had done this good for the sailors, that as we could not send our cocoa and sugar to the continent, the government had made that addition to the allowance of the men.

We now tacked and stood over towards the Corsican shore, passing a small vessel, he was very anxious for me to hail her for news; I told him we could not get near enough for that purpose, as she was to windward crossing us on the opposite tack, we were then at table; he whispered me to fire at her and bring her down; I expressed my surprise at his request as it would denationalize her (referring to his Milan decree) he pinched my ear and laughed, remarking that the treaty of Utrecht directs, that when vessels are boarded it shall be done out of gunshot, it was on this occasion, he said, England was not prepared for the steps he took in retaliation, upon her blockading an entire line of coast from the river Elbe to Brest, it was that which forced him to take possession of Holland. America behaved with spirit, he said, adding, he thought their state correspondence was very well managed and contained much sound reasoning.

I asked him if he issued his Milan decrees for the purpose of forcing America to quarrel with us. He said he was angry with America for suffering her flag to be denationalized; he spoke long on this subject, and said that America had justice on her side; he rather expected America to invade Mexico, he said the expedition against Copenhagen was most unjust, and in every point of view bad policy; and, that after all, we only took a few vessels that were of no use to us, that the gross injustice of attacking a weaker nation, without a cause and without a declaration of war, did us infinite harm. I observed that it was at that time believed that their fleet was sold to him.

In speaking of Toulon, he remarked that he found great inconvenience in being obliged to complete the provisions and stores after the ships went out of the inner harbours, as it gave information of his intentions to British cruisers, to avoid this, he sent the *Rivoli* out from Venice on a camel, with her guns, stores, and provisions on board, he meant to form an establishment for building men-of-war at Bouc, near the mouth of the Rhone, instead of at Toulon, the timber for which was to be brought there by a canal from the Rhone, and that he intended to make Toulon a port of equipment.

In speaking of Cherbourg, he described the basin cut out of the solid rock, with docks for ships, executed by his orders, and drew with a pencil, on a plan I have of the town, a line of fortifications, erected for its defence, against any expedition from England, which it seemed he expected the entrance is mined at each side, the Empress Marie Louisa visited Cherbourg (when he was at Dresden) at the completion of the works last year. He said he had in his possession what would be invaluable to England, spoke of the weak and strong points of the empire; some remarks arising from this observation, he said France is nothing without Antwerp, for while Brest and Toulon are blockaded a fleet can be equipped there, wood is brought from Poland; he never would consent to give it up, having sworn at his coronation not to diminish France. He had the Elbe sounded and surveyed carefully, and found that it was as favourable as the Scheldt for great naval establishments near Hamburgh.

He told me his plans for the navy were on a gigantic scale, he would have had three hundred sail of the line; I observed that it was impossible he could man half the number. He said the naval conscription, with the enlistment of foreigners, which he could have from all parts of Europe, would supply men enough for the whole of his navy, that the Zuyder sea is particularly well calculated for exercising conscripts. Having expressed some doubts as to the merits of his conscript sailors, he said I was mistaken, and asked my opinion of the Toulon fleet, which I had had frequent opportunities of seeing manoeuvre in the presence of our fleet, he begged I would tell him frankly what I thought of it.

The conscripts were trained or exercised, for two years, in schooners and small craft, and his best officers and seamen appointed to command them, that they were constantly at sea, either to protect the coasting trade or exercising; he did not calculate on their becoming perfect seamen by these means, but intended to have sent squadrons out to the East and West Indies, not for the purpose of attacking the colonies, but for perfecting the men and annoying, at the same time, the commerce of England; he calculated upon losing some ships; but said he should be able to spare them, that they would be well paid for. Whilst on this subject, he surprised me by explaining to Baron Koller (and that very well) a very nice point of seamanship, *viz*., that of keeping a ship clear of her anchor in a tide-way.

He admired much the regularity with which the duty of the ship was carried on, everything being so well timed, and, above all, the respect observed by the different ranks of officers to each other, and to the quarter deck, he thought this most essential to good discipline, and was not surprised that we were so tenacious of the slightest deviation from it, that he endeavoured to introduce this into the French navy, but could not drive it into the heads of his captains. The wind still continuing to the east-ward, with a heavy sea, we stood in, to get well in with the Corsican shore, having carried away the leech ropes of the fore and main topsails; we repaired them aloft, close reefed them, and sent down top-gallant-yards and royal masts, there being now every appearance of bad weather. I mentioned my intention, if the gale increased, of anchoring at Bastia, Napoleon seemed most desirous that we should, in that case, anchor at Ajacio, I explained to him that it was much out of our course; he proposed Calvi, with which he was perfectly acquainted, mentioning the depth of water, with other remarks on the harbour, &c., which convinced me he would have made us an excellent pilot had we touched there.

This evening we fell in, and exchanged numbers, with the *Berwick*, *Aigle*, and *Alemene*, with a convoy; I invited Sir John Lewis and Captain Coglan to dine with me. When they came on board I presented them to Napoleon; he asked them various questions about their ships, their sailing, and other qualities. Captain Coglan was not a little surprised by his asking him if he were not an Irishman and a Roman Catholic. All this night we carried sail to get in shore, the *Aigle* and *Alemene* keeping company. At daylight we saw the town of Calvi bearing south, Napoleon was on deck earlier than usual, he seemed in high spirits, looked most earnestly at the shore, asking the officers questions relative to landing places, &c. As we closed with the shore, the wind moderated. During the bad weather Napoleon remained constantly on deck, and was not in the least affected by the motion of the ship this was not the case, however, with his attendants, who suffered a good deal.

The wind now coming off the land, we hauled close in shore; Napoleon took great delight in examining it with his glass, and told us many anecdotes of his younger days. We rounded a bold rocky cape, within two or three cables length. Napoleon, addressing himself to Baron Roller, said he thought a walk on shore would do them good, and proposed landing to explore the cliffs. The Baron whispered that he knew him too well to trust him on such an excursion, and begged me not to listen to his suggestion. We now hauled in towards the gulf of San Fiorenza, fired a gun, and brought to a *felucca* from Genoa, who informed us that Sir Edward Pellew, the commander-in-chief, and fleet were lying there. We then shaped our course for Cape Corso, which we passed in the night. In the morning we tacked and stood towards Capraja Isle, and observing colours flying at the castle, stood close in and hove to. A deputation came off from the island requesting me to take possession of it, and informing me that there was a French garrison in the castle.

I accordingly sent Lieutenant Smith with a party of seamen to hoist the British colours for its protection. Napoleon held a long conversation with the members of the deputation, who expressed the utmost surprise at finding their Emperor on board an English man-of-war. Having now made all sail, and shaped our course for Elba, Napoleon became very impatient to see it, and asked if we had every sail set. I told him we had all that could be of any use.

He said, "were you in chase of an enemy's frigate should you make more sail?"

I looked, and seeing that the starboard top-gallant stern-sail was not set, I observed, that if I were in chase of an enemy I should certainly carry it. He replied if it could be of use in that case it might be so now. I mention this anecdote to show what a close observer he was, that in fact nothing escaped him.

When the man stationed at the mast-head hailed the deck that Elba was right ahead, he became exceedingly impatient, went forward to the forecastle, and as soon as the land could be seen from the deck, was very particular in enquiring what colours were flying on the batteries. He seemed to doubt the garrison having given in their adhesion to the Bourbons, and it appears not without some reason, as they had, in fact, only done so during the preceding forty-eight hours, so that if we had had a fair wind I should have found the island in the hands of the enemy, and consequently must have taken my charge to the commander-in-chief, who would, no doubt, have ordered us to England.

On nearing Elba, General Druot, with Comte Clam (*aid-de-camp* to Prince Schwartzenberg) and Lieutenant Hastings, the first lieutenant of the *Undaunted*, were sent on shore, commissioned by Napoleon to take possession of the island. Colonel Campbell accompanied them. They were conducted to the house of General Dalkeme, who had received orders from the Provisional Government only two days before, in consequence of which, he and his troops had given in their adhesion to Louis XVIII. and hoisted the white flag. The general expressed his desire to do whatever should be agreeable to the Emperor.

May 3rd, 1814, one part of Druot's instructions from Napoleon, mentioned his desire to receive the names of all officers, non-commissioned officers, and privates, who would wish to enter into his service. He desired also a deputation of the principal inhabitants to come off to him. At about eight o'clock, p.m., we anchored at the entrance of the harbour, and soon after the deputation waited upon Napoleon; there had been originally about three thousand troops, but desertion, and the discharge of discontented foreigners, had reduced the number to about seven hundred. The island had been in a state of revolt for several weeks, in consequence of which, the troops were shut up in the fortifications, which surround the town of Porto Ferragio. During the night, an Austrian officer was sent off in one of my boats to Piombino, to invite a renewal of communication, and obtain news, &c. This was done by a letter from the Commissioners to the Commandant, who, however, politely declined communicating with us, at the same time stating that he had written to his superior for permission to do so.

May 4th, Napoleon was on deck at daylight, and talked for two hours with the harbour master, who had come on board to take charge of the ship as pilot, questioning him minutely about the anchorage, fortifications, &c. At six, we weighed and made sail into the harbour; anchored at half-past six near the mole head, and moored ship, hoisted out all the boats and sent some of the baggage on shore. At eight the Emperor asked me for a boat, as he intended to take a walk on the opposite side of the bay, and requested me to go with him. He wore a great coat and a round hat. Comte Bertrand, Colonel Campbell, and Colonel Vincent (chief engineer) went with us; Baron Roller declined doing so. When halfway he remarked he was without a sword, and soon afterwards asked if the peasants of Tuscany were addicted to assassination.

We walked for about two hours. The peasants, taking us for Englishmen, cried "*Viva*," which seemed to displease him; we returned on board to breakfast. He afterwards fixed upon a flag for Elba, requesting me to remain while he did so. He had a book with all the ancient and modern flags of Tuscany; he asked my opinion of that which he had chosen, it was a white flag with a red band running diagonally through it, with three bees on the band (the bees were in his arms as Emperor of France.) He then requested me to allow the ship's tailor to make two, one of them to be hoisted on the batteries at one o'clock. At two, p.m., the barge was manned, he begged me to show him the way down the side of the vessel, which I did, and was soon followed by the Emperor, General Koller, Comte Bertrand, and Comte Clam. The yards being manned we fired a royal salute, as did two French corvettes which were at that time lying in the harbour.

The ship was surrounded by boats with the principal inhabitants, and bands of music on board. The air resounded with shouts of "*Vive l'Empereur, Vive Napoleon!*" On landing, he was received by the prefect, the clergy, and all the authorities, and the keys were presented to him on a plate, upon which he made a complimentary speech to the prefect, the people welcoming him with loud acclamations. We proceeded to the church through a double file of soldiers, and from thence to the Hotel de Ville, where the principal inhabitants were assembled, with several of whom he conversed. Remarking an old soldier in the crowd (he was a sergeant, I believe, and wore the order of the Legion of Honour) he called him to him, and seemed delighted to see him, spoke to him by name, and recollected having given him that "decoration" on the field of battle at Eylau. The old soldier shed tears; the idea of being remembered by his Emperor fairly overcame him. He felt, I doubt not, it was the proudest day of his life. Napoleon afterwards mounted a horse, and attended by a dozen persons, visited some of the outworks; having, before leaving the ship, invited me to dine with him at seven o'clock. I ordered all my wine and stock to be landed for his use, the island being destitute of provisions of that sort.

May 5th, at four a.m., I was awoke by shouts of "*Vive l'Empereur,*" and drums beating; Napoleon was already up, and going on foot over the fortifications, magazines, and storehouses. At ten he returned to breakfast, and at two mounted his horse, and I accompanied him two leagues into the country. He examined various country houses, and gave money to all the poor we met on the road. At seven he returned to dinner. I should remark that before leaving the *Undaunted*, Napoleon requested that a party of fifty marines might accompany him and remain on shore, but this he afterwards changed to an officer and two sergeants, one of whom, O'Gorum (one of the bravest and best soldiers I ever met with, and whom he had taken a great fancy to) he selected to sleep outside the door of his bedchamber, on a mattress, with his clothes and sword on. A *valet de chambre* slept on another mattress in the same place, and if Napoleon lay down during the day, the sergeant remained in the antechamber.

May 6th, at six o'clock, we crossed the bay in my barge and found horses waiting for us. We rode to Riou to see the famous iron mountains. We visited several mines, and likewise a temple built by the Romans, and dedicated by them to Jupiter. The road to the latter is highly romantic and beautiful, but it is difficult of access, being situated on the summit of a steep and lofty mountain; this obliged us to dismount, and we walked through a thick covert of beautiful trees and shrubs till we arrived at the temple. We saw also a small museum very nicely kept, and containing many fine specimens of the ores of the adjoining mines, two or three of which Napoleon presented me with. He expressed a wish to see the principal mine, and when everything was prepared, asked Baron Koller, myself, and one or two of the party to accompany him, which they politely declined; I, however, accepted his invitation. Two guides, with flambeaux, accompanied us.

When we arrived at the middle of, what appeared to me, an immense cavern, the guides suddenly struck the ground with their flambeaux, and all around became instantly and splendidly illuminated. At the moment I expected an explosion; Napoleon may have thought so too, but he very coolly took a pinch of snuff and desired me to follow him. At Riou, *Te Deum* was chaunted, I suppose for the first time, as the officiating priest did not seem to understand his business. In passing through Riou a salute was fired, and he was received with loud acclamations and cries of "*Vive l'Empereur.*" The people seemed very anxious to see him. Several old women presented petitions, and numbers pressed forward to kiss his hand. At five, we embarked in the barge and crossed the harbour to Porto Ferraggio; at seven we sat down to dinner. He spoke of his intention of taking possession of Pianosa, a small island without inhabitants, about ten miles from Elba.

He said, "*Toute l'Europe dira, que j'ai deja fait une conquête;*" already he had plans in agitation for conveying water from the mountains to the city. It appears always to have been considered by him of the first importance to have a supply of good water for the inhabitants of towns, and upon this occasion, it was evidently the first thing that occupied his mind, having almost immediately requested me to go with him in the barge in search of water. One day exploring for this purpose, he remarked the boats of the *Undaunted* in a small creek watering; he said he was quite sure that good water was to be had there, I asked him why he thought so; he said, depend upon it, sailors always know where to find the best, there are no better judges. We landed at the place he desired to taste the water; Jack made the rim of his hat into what is called a cocked hat, and filled it with water, Napoleon was amused at the contrivance, tasted the water and pronounced it excellent. The cleanliness of the streets he also thought of the greatest importance, and requested I would allow the carpenter of the ship to go to him (having told him he was a tolerable good engineer) that he might consult him about forcing the sea water, by means of pumps, to the summit of the hill. Porto Ferraggio is built on the side of a hill, crowned by strong works for the defence of the town. I believe he afterwards abandoned his sea water plan, which would have been attended with great expense. He had also plans for a palace and a country house, and a house for Princess Pauline, stables, a *lazaretto* and quarantine ground, about the latter he asked my opinion.

May 7th, from four till ten, a.m., Napoleon was employed visiting the town and fortifications; after breakfast he again embarked in the barge, and visited the different storehouses round the harbour. In making excursions into the country he was accompanied by a dozen officers and the captain of the *gens d'armerie*, and one of the Fouriers de Palais always rode before, and sometimes a party of *gens d'armes* a pied.

After taking our places in the barge, some of the party kept their hats off, he desired them to put them on, remarking, "*nous sommes ici ensemble en soldats.*" The fishing for the tunny is carried on here by one of the richest inhabitants, who, from poverty, has amassed a large fortune; he employs a great number of the poor and has considerable influence. The removal of his stores to a very inferior building, to make way for a stable for the Emperor's horses, is likely to give great offence.

May 8th, the *Curacoa*, Captain Towers, arrived with Mr. Locker, secretary to Sir Edward Pellew, commander-in-chief, he requested an audience, to present to the Emperor a copy of the treaty of peace. Napoleon received Mr. Locker very graciously, and seemed to read the treaty with deep interest. Baron Roller, Comte Bertrand, Druot, General Dalheme, &c.; Colonel Campbell, Captain Towers, and myself were pre sent. Having read it, he folded and returned it to Mr. Locker, expressing his obligations to the commander-in-chief.

May 9th, Baron Roller having demanded an audience, took

leave of the Emperor and embarked in the *Curacoa* for Genoa. I, this day, accompanied Napoleon to Longone, where we lunched amid repeated cries of "*Vive l'Empereur.*" Longone is a place of considerable strength, the works are regular, the bay is small, but there is safe anchorage within. Many old people presented petitions, and girls brought flowers, which he accepted with much condescension, talking to all, but particularly to those that were pretty. A young lad fell on his knees before him, either to ask charity or merely as a mark of respect, he turned to Colonel Campbell and said, "*Ah! je connais bien les Italiens, c'est l'education des moines, on ne voit pas cela parmi le peuple du nord.*"

On proceeding a little farther we met two well dressed young women, who saluted him with compliments, one of them, the youngest, told him with great ease and gaiety, that she had been invited to the ball at Longone two days before, but as the Emperor did not attend it, as was expected, she had remained at home. Instead of returning by the same road, he turned off by goat-paths to examine the coast, humming Italian airs, which he does very often, and seemed quite in spirits; he expressed his fondness for music, and remarked that this reminded him of passing Mont St. Bernard, and of a conversation he had had with a young peasant upon that occasion; the man, he said, not knowing who he was, spoke freely of the happiness of those who possessed a good house, and a number of cattle, &c.; he made him enumerate his greatest wants and desires, and afterwards sent for him and gave him all that he had described, "*cela m'a couté 60,000 francs.*"

May 10th, Napoleon rode to the top of the highest hill above Porto Ferraggio, from whence we could perceive the sea at four different points, and apparently not an English mile in a straight line in any direction from the spot where we stood. After surveying it for some time, he turned round and laughed, "*Eh! mon isle est bien petite.*"

On the top of this hill is a small chapel and a house, where a hermit had resided until his death. Someone remarked that it would require more than common devotion to induce persons to attend service there. *"Oui, oui, le Prâtre peut dire autant de Bêtises qu'il veut."* On the evening of the 9th, after his return from Longone, he entered upon the subject of the armies and their operations at the close of the last campaign, and continued it for half an hour, until he rose from table.

After passing into the presence chamber, the conversation again turned on the campaign, his own policy, the Bourbons, &c., and he continued talking with great animation till midnight, remaining for three hours on his legs. He described the operations against the Allies as always in his favour, while the numbers were in any sort of proportion, that in one affair against the Prussians, who were infinitely the best, he had only seven hundred infantry *en tirailleurs*, with two thousand cavalry and three battalions of his guards in reserve, against double their numbers.

The instant those old soldiers showed themselves the affair was decided. He praised General Blucher, *"le vieux diable m'a toujours attaqué avec la même vigueur, s'il etoit battu, un instant après il se montrait prêt pour le combat."*

He then described his last march from Arcis to Brienne, said that he knew Swartzenberg would not stand to fight him, and that he hoped to destroy half his army. Upon his retreat, he had already taken an immense quantity of baggage and guns. When it was reported to him that the enemy had crossed the Aube to Vitry, he was induced to halt, he would not, however, credit it, till General Gerard assured him that he saw twenty thousand infantry, he was overjoyed at this assurance and immediately returned to St. Dizier, where he attacked Wintzingerode's cavalry, which he considered the advance guard of Swartzenberg's army, drove them before him a whole day like sheep, at full gallop, took fifteen hundred or two thousand prisoners, and some light pieces of artillery; but to his surprise did not see any army, and again halted. His best information led him to believe, that instead of retreating to Sangres they had returned to Troyes. Accordingly he marched in that direction, and then ascertained, after a loss of three days, that the two armies of Swartzenberg and Blucher had marched upon Paris; he then ordered forced marches, and went forward himself (with his suite and carriages) on horseback, day and night, never were he or his friends more gay and confident; he knew, he said, all the workmen of Paris would fight for him, what could the Allies do with such a force? The National Guards had only to barricade the streets with casks and it would be impossible for them to advance before he arrived to their assistance.

At eight, a.m., a few leagues from Paris, he met a column of stragglers, who stared at him and he at them, "*qu'est ce que c'est cela?*" he demanded; they stopped and seemed stupefied "*quoi! c'est l'Empereur.*" They informed him they had retreated through Paris; he was still confident of success. His army burnt with desire to attack the enemy and drive them out of the capital; he knew very well what Swartzenberg would risk, and the composition of the allied army compared with his own, that he never would hazard a general battle with Paris in his rear, that he would take the defensive position on the other side; he would have engaged them in various points for two or three hours, then have marched with his thirty battalions of guards and eighty pieces of cannon, himself at the head, upon one part of the enemy's force, nothing could withstand that, but although his inferiority of numbers would not enable him to hope for a complete victory, yet he should succeed in killing a great number of the enemy, and forcing them to abandon Paris and its neighbourhood, what he would afterwards do must depend on various circumstances.

Who could have supposed that the senate would have dishonoured themselves by assembling under the force of 20,000 foreign bayonets (a timidity unexampled in history) and that a man who owed everything to him who had been his *aide-de-camp*, and attached to him for twenty years, would have betrayed him! Still it was but a faction, which ruled Paris under the influence of the enemy's, force; the rest of the nation was for him, the army would, almost to a man, continue to fight for him, but with so great an inferiority in point of number, it would be certain destruction to many of his friends and a war for years; he preferred, therefore, sacrificing his own rights. It was not for the sake of a crown that he had continued the war, it was for the glory of France, and not for the sake of plans which he saw no prospect of realizing, he wished to have made France the first nation in the world, now it was at an end, "*j'ai abdiqué, à présent je suis un homme mort!*"

He repeated the latter phrase several times. In remarking on his confidence in his own troops and his "*Vieille Garde,*" and the want of union among the Allies, he referred to Colonel Campbell, to say candidly if it was not so, "*dites, Campbell, franchement, n'est ce pas vrai.*" Colonel Campbell told him it was, that he had never seen any very considerable portion of the French army, but everyone spoke of the Emperor and his "*Vieille Garde,*" as if there were something more than human about them, that the inferiority which he conceived of Swartzenberg's army, was justly founded, they had no confidence in themselves or on their allies, each party thought he did too much, and his allies too little, and that they were half beaten before they closed with the French. He sneered at Marmont's anxiety for his life, "*fut il jamais rien si naive que cette capitulation;*" he wished to protect his person but deserted, leaving him and the whole of his comrades open to the surprise of the enemy, for it was his corps which covered the whole front. The night previous, Marmont said to him, "*pour mon corps d'armee j'en réponds,*" so he might.

The officers and soldiers were enraged when they found what had been done, eight thousand infantry, three thousand cavalry, and sixty pieces of cannon. "*Voila l'histoire,*" he animadverted on his conduct before Paris, saying, whoever heard of such a thing, two hundred pieces of artillery in the Champ de Mars, and only sixty on the heights of Montmartre. General Dalheme asked whether he had not fought with vigour. This was nearly all that passed at that time. After accompanying him into another room he resumed the conversation, enlarging upon the general state of this army and the policy of France. He seemed to repent his abdication, and said, that had he known that it was owing to the treachery of Augereau only, that his army fell back behind Lyons, he would have united his own to it, even after Marmont's capitulation. He animadverted strongly on the conduct of Augereau, yet he met him with all the kindness of a friend. The first idea of his defection struck him after separating from him on the road between Valence and Lyons.

The spirit of the troops was such, that he durst not remain among them, for on his arrival, many old officers and soldiers came up to him weeping, and said, they were betrayed by Augereau, and requested Napoleon would put himself at their head; he had an army of thirty thousand fine men, many of them from the army of Spain, which ought to have kept its ground against the Austrians. He again spoke of Marmont's defection, that it was reported to him in the morning, but he did not believe it—that he rode out and met Berthier, who confirmed it from an undoubted source. He referred to the armistice between Lord Castlereagh and Talleyrand, that he thought the Allies were pursuing a bad policy with regard to France, by reducing her so much, for it would wound the pride of every man there; they might have left them much more power without any risk, and yet without being on an equality with several other powers.

France had no longer any fleet or colonies—a peace would not restore ships or St. Domingo. Poland no longer existed, nor Venice; these went to aggrandize Russia and Austria. Spain, which is the natural enemy of Great Britain more so than of France, was incapable of doing anything as an ally, if to these sacrifices were added, that of a disadvantageous treaty of commerce with Great Britain, the people of France would not remain tranquil under it, "*pas même six mois, après que les puissances étrangeres, quitterent Paris.*"

He then remarked that a month had already elapsed, and the King of France had not yet come over to the people who had placed him on the throne. He said, now England would do as she pleased, the other powers were nothing in comparison, "*pour vingt années au moins, aucune puissance, ne peut faire guerre contre l'Angleterre et elle fera ce qu'elle veut.*"

Holland would be entirely subservient to her, the armistice gave no information as to the ships at Antwerp or in the Texel, "*le brave Verheul, se défend toujours,*" (this admiral commanded the ships at Antwerp.)

He then enumerated the number of ships he had in each of the ports, that in three or four years he would have had three hundred sail of the line, "*quelle différence pour la France!*" with many other remarks in the same strain.

Colonel Campbell remarked, but we do not know why your Majesty wishes to annihilate us, he laughed, and replied, "*si j'avais été ministre d' Angleterre jaurais taché d'enfaire la plus grande puissance du monde.*"

Napoleon frequently spoke of the invasion of England, that he never intended to attempt it without a superiority of fleet to protect the flotilla, this superiority would have been attained for a few days, by leading ours out to the West Indies, and suddenly returning, if it arrived three or four days before ours in the channel it would be sufficient. The flotilla would immediately push out, accompanied by the fleet, and the landing might take place on any part of the coast, as he would march direct to London; he preferred the coast of Kent, but that must have depended on wind and weather; he should have placed himself at the disposal of the naval officers and pilots, to land the troops wherever they thought they could do so with the greatest security and in the least time. He had 100,000 men, each of the flotilla having boats to land them, artillery and cavalry would soon have followed, and the whole could have reached London in three days; he armed the flotilla merely as a false attack, to lead us to suppose that he intended them to fight their way across the channel, but it was only to deceive us. It was observed that we expected to be treated with great severity in case of his succeeding, and he was asked what he would have done had he arrived in London; he said, it was a difficult question to answer, for a people with spirit and energy like the English, was not to be subdued, even by taking their capital. He would certainly have separated Ireland from Great Britain, and the occupying the capital would have been a death blow to our funds, credit and commerce; he asked us to say frankly, whether we were not alarmed at his preparation for invading England.

He entered into a long conversation with Comte Druot (who was with Admiral Villeneuve in the action with Sir Robert Calder) as to his operations, Comte Druot, said Admiral Villeneuve did not want either zeal or talents, but he was impressed with a great idea of the British navy—that after the action, he was entreated by all the officers to pursue the British squadron and to renew the action. He said, that about the end of the campaign of 1804, before England had seized the Spanish galleons, and before he had obtained from Spain an entire and frank co-operation, having then no other auxiliary but the Dutch, he wished to run the Toulon fleet through the Straits, unite it to six sail of the line at Rochfort, the Brest fleet which consisted of twenty-three sail of the line, and with this combined force to appear before Boulogne, there to be joined by the Dutch fleet, thus securing the passage and landing of his troops. He said he was diverted from his intentions of invasion by the Austrians.

At the death of Admiral de la Touche Treville, one of his most able admirals, Villeneuve was appointed commander-in-chief at Toulon, and hoisted his flag in the *Bucentaur*, his squadron consisted of four eighty-gun ships, eight seventy-fours, six frigates, and seven thousand troops. On the 30th March, 1805, Admiral Villeneuve sailed from Toulon, and on the 7th April was before Carthegena, waiting a reinforcement of six Spanish sail of the line, these ships not being ready, he pursued his course about the middle of April, appeared before Gibraltar and chased Sir John Orde, who, with five sail of the line, was before Cadiz. Admiral Villeneuve was joined by a seventy-four and two corvettes, and by Admiral Gravina with six sail of the line and two thousand troops, making eighteen sail of the line in all.

The 9th of May, Villeneuve opened his sealed orders and gave Admiral Gravina his instructions, which were to separate with his squadron, reinforce the garrison of Porto Rico and Havannah, and rejoin him at a prescribed rendezvous. Villeneuve anchored at Martinique on the 14th May, and heard that Admiral Misiessy had just left the West Indies; he sailed from Rochfort the 11th January, his squadron consisting of six sail of the line and three frigates, and three thousand troops, his flag-ship the *Majestieux*. Napoleon said, he was visiting the fortresses on the Rhine when he wrote the orders for these expeditions. The first to reinforce Martinique and Guadaloupe, take Dominica and St. Lucia; the second to take Surinam and its dependencies, and strengthen St. Domingo; the third to St. Helena. It was before he quitted Milan, to visit the departments of the east, that he learnt the return of the Rochfort squadron, though he blamed the precipitation with which Dominique had been abandoned.

He saw in this fortunate cruise the advantage he had gained, he felicitated himself in having concealed the secret of the destination of Villeneuve, still he was uneasy about Nelson. In his dispatch, written at the moment of his departure from Milan, he said, it is uncertain what Nelson intends doing, it is very possible the English, having sent a strong squadron to the East Indies, have ordered Nelson to America. I am, however, of opinion, that he is still in Europe; the most natural supposition is, that he has returned to England to refit and turn his men over to other vessels, as some of his ships want docking; he impressed on the mind of the Minister of Marine the importance he attached to Villeneuve's having the means of victualling his fleet at Ferrol; he said, with respect to the Rochfort squadron, the English will, no doubt, send a squadron after them you must not calculate upon what it is the duty of the admiralty to do, one hundred thousand men at Boulogne, seven sail of the line in the Texel, with an army of thirty thousand men and a fleet of twenty-two sail of the line at Brest.

It may happen that Villeneuve will return suddenly, but he might also direct his course to India or to Jamaica, what responsibility then weighs on the heads of the Ministers, if they allow months to pass without sending a force to protect the colonies; it is scarcely probable England could, at any time, assemble sixty-five sail of the line, you should send to Villeneuve the moment he arrives at Ferrol, as nothing gives greater courage and clears the ideas so well as knowing the position of the enemy. It is true, the English have one hundred and eleven sail of the line, of which three are guard ships, sixteen prison ships or hospitals, there remain then ninety-two, out of which twenty are under repair (that is not ready for sea) there remains then seventy-two, the disposition of which is, probably, eight or ten in India, three or four at Jamaica, three or four at Barbados, making sixteen or eighteen, leaving fifty-four or fifty-six with which it is necessary to blockade Cadix, Ferrol, and Brest, and to follow Villeneuve and Misiessy.

The following is the state of our force twenty-two at Brest, fifteen at Cadiz, twelve at Ferrol, twenty with Admiral Villeneuve, one at Lorient, five with Misiessy, total seventy-four; the fifteen at Cadiz occupy but six English, deduct the nine from seventy-four, there remains sixty-five, which I can unite. It is scarcely possible that the English can, at any time, assemble sixty-five. Villeneuve having sailed to the West Indies, was pursued by Nelson, he left the anchorage at Martinique on the 21st May, captured a convoy off Barbados and off the Azores, fell in with and captured a privateer, with a rich prize, a galleon; he was afterwards reinforced by Admiral Magon with two sail of the line, and received from him instructions to proceed off Ferrol, when he would be reinforced by five sail of the line under the command of Rear-Admiral Gourgon, and six sail of the line, Spaniards, under the command of Admiral Grandelina, and a third squadron, under the command of Rear Admiral Lallemande, consisting of five sail of the line (formerly under the command of Misiessy.)

It was with this mass of about forty sail of the line, that Villeneuve, driving away Admiral Cornwallis from Brest, would necessarily open the passage for Admiral Gantheaume, who had twenty-two sail of the line, and form at the entrance of the channel sixty-two sail of the line, six three-deckers, nine eighty-gun ships, and forty-seven seventy fours; they were to cover the two thousand two hundred and eighty-three transports of which the flotilla consisted; such was his plan, the execution of which was defeated by Villeneuve, who, after the action with Sir Robert

Calder, went into Vigo, landed his wounded, and leaving three sail of the line there ran into Corunna, where he was reinforced by six sail of the line French, and ten sail of the line Spanish, making thirty-one sail of the line.

Napoleon was at Boulogne at this time, and learned from England the situations of the different squadrons, he ordered Gantheaume to anchor in Bertheaume bay (Brest) and to be ready to join Villeneuve with the twenty-two sail of the line, three of them three-deckers. The 21st of August, he anchored in Bertheaume bay. The 10th of August, wind easterly, Villeneuve having been reinforced by the French and Spanish squadrons under Gourgon, Gravina and Grandelina, anchored in the bay of Arras near Ferrol, and put to sea the 13th. Nothing being then in sight, he first steered N.W., suddenly changed his course to the southward, out of sight of land, cruised four days off Cape St. Vincent, and entered Cadiz the 21st, the very day that he was expected at Brest; Lord Collingwood was before Cadiz with four sail of the line, was surprised and narrowly escaped.

Whilst this was going on, Admiral Lallemande, with four sail of the line, was cruising in the Bay of Biscay, his orders were to cruise to a certain period, then to wait in a particular latitude for orders, and if none reached him, then he was to proceed to Vigo, the 13th, in order to reinforce Villeneuve, he executed punctually his orders, and anchored on the 16th, two days after Villeneuve had sailed; and although he expected this reinforcement, he left no orders for Lallemande, compromising by this extraordinary conduct the safety of the squadron. Lallemande, finding no orders, put to sea again, and cruised till the 24th December, he took a fifty gun ship, a sloop of war, anchored at Rochfort the 24th of December. Napoleon was at Boulogne, the anniversary of his birthday, when he learned from England the certainty of Villeneuve arriving at Cadiz, he was furious, saying it was treason. Villeneuve, before leaving Ferrol, said that he was going to Brest, and even wrote to Lallemande, who was to meet him at Vigo, and notwithstanding that he expected this squadron at Vigo, he passed the harbour without sending in. Napoleon ordered the Minister of Marine to make a report of his proceedings.

May 26th, Napoleon had been so long expecting his troops and baggage, horses, &c., that he began at length to show signs of impatience, and to suspect the good faith of the French government, but when I informed him that our transports were engaged for that purpose, and might shortly be expected at Elba, he seemed satisfied, complimented us on our generosity, and added, that had he known our ships were to bring his troops, he should not have had a moment's uneasiness. I dined with Napoleon the following day. While at table, a servant announced one of my officers, who wanted to see me, it was an officer whom I had stationed at a signal post, established by me on a commanding height. He reported seven sail in the N.W. quarter, standing towards the island. I had no doubt from this number, and the course these vessels were steering, that they were the long expected transports, Napoleon almost instantly rose from table, and I accompanied him to his garden, which with his house occupies the highest part of the works, and has a commanding view of the sea towards Italy, and the coast of France.

Full of anxiety, he stepped at the end of every walk, and looked eagerly for the vessels, we walked till it was quite dark, he was very communicative, and his conversation highly interesting. It was now near midnight I told him with a good night-glass I should be able to see them, as from the breeze they had, they could not be very far from the island; he brought me a very fine night-glass made by Donaldson, which enabled me to see the vessels distinctly, they were lying to. He was much pleased, and in the highest spirits wished me good night. At four in the morning he was out again giving orders, I was awaked by the beating of drums, and cries of "*Vive l'Empereur.*"

He ordered the harbour master and pilots out to the transports, made arrangements for the comfort of his troops, and provided stables for one hundred horses. At about seven o'clock, the troops were landed, and paraded before Napoleon, who addressed every officer, and private. They appeared quite delighted at again seeing their Emperor. Among the officers were several Poles, remarkably fine young men. At eight o'clock, I ordered half the crew of the *Undaunted*, to be sent on board the transport, and by four o'clock, the whole of the baggage, carriages, horses, &c,, were landed, and the transport ready for sea. During the whole of the operation he was on the quay, in the midst of an excessively hot sun. When I informed him that everything was landed, and that the transports had completed their water, and were ready for sea, he expressed surprise, and said, pointing to some Italian sailors, those fellows would have been eight days doing what yours have done in as many hours, besides they would have broken my horses legs, not one of whom has received a scratch. General Cambrone, who came in command of the troops, remained in conversation with Napoleon the whole time. At four he mounted his horse, and rode into the country, and returned to dinner at seven.

At half-past seven he rose from table, and I accompanied him to his garden, where we walked till half-past eleven. It was during our conversation this night, that I told him it was generally thought in England, that he intended to rebuild Jerusalem, and that what gave rise to the supposition was, his convoking the Sanhedrim of the Jews at Paris. He laughed and said, the Sanhedrim was convoked for other purposes it collected Jews who came from all parts of Europe, but particularly from Poland, and from them, he obtained information of the state of Poland. He added, that they gave him much useful information, that they were well informed as to the real state of the country on every point, and possessed all the information he wanted, and which he was able to turn to account, and found to be perfectly correct. Great numbers came to Paris on that occasion, amongst them several Jews from England.

In talking of his marshals, he seemed to regret that he had not allowed some of them to retire; he said they wanted retirement, he ought to have made a batch of young men who would have been attached to him; like Massena, he considered Gouvion St. Cyr, one of his best soldiers. He said Ney was a man that lived on fire, that he would go into the canon's mouth, if he was ordered; but he was not a man of talent or education. Marmont was a good soldier, but a weak man. Soult was a talented and a good soldier. Bernadotte, he said, had behaved ill on one occasion, and that he ought to have been tried by a court-martial; he did not interfere or influence in any way his election by the Swedes.

He had a high opinion of Junot (who stood at his side when writing a dispatch on a drum-head, on the field of battle, during which time a shot passed, turning up the earth about them, Junot remarked that it was very apropos, as he wanted sand to dry his ink). The following morning I requested an interview to take leave, on my sailing from Elba to join the commander-in-chief at Genoa. He was alone at the time he seemed affected, and requested me to prolong my stay at Elba, and asked me if the wind was fair for Genoa. He said, "you are the first Englishman I have been acquainted with"; and spoke in a flattering manner of England. He said he felt under great obligations to Sir Edward Pellew, and requested I would assure him of his gratitude, for the attentions shown him; hoped when the war with America was terminated, I would pay him a visit.

I told him, I had that morning breakfasted with the Comte de Moncabri, on board the *Dryade* frigate, that he informed me of the Prince of Esling having had a dispute with Sir Edward Pellew, and that the government, had in consequence, some intention of removing him from the command at Toulon. He remarked, that he was one of his best marshals, a man of superior talent; but that his health was bad in consequence of bursting a blood vessel. I said, it was understood that he was so much displeased with the conduct of the Prince of Esling in the Peninsula, that he had ordered him to Barege. He replied that I was greatly mistaken, that at the time he alluded to, his health was very delicate, and his physicians recommended him to go to Nice, the place of his birth, and that after his recovery, he gave him the command at Toulon, which was just then vacant. I requested he would allow me to present Lieutenant Bailey, the agent of transports, who had been appointed to embark his guards, etc. at Savona. He thanked Lieutenant Bailey for the attention paid to his troops, and the care which had been taken of his horses, and remarked how extraordinary it was, that no accident had happened to them (there were ninety three) either in the embarkation or disembarkation, and highly complimented him on his skill and attention, and added, that our sailors exceeded even the opinion which he had long since formed of them.

During this conversation Napoleon gave a remarkable proof of his retentive memory, and of his information on subjects connected with naval matters. Lieutenant Bailey informed him, that after the guards had embarked, a violent gale of wind arose, with a heavy sea, which at one time threatened the destruction of the transports, and that he considered Savona a dangerous anchorage. Napoleon remarked, that if he had gone to a small bay (I think it was Vado) near Savona, he might have lain there in perfect safety.

He requested me to inform the commander-in-chief, how much he was satisfied with Lieutenant Bailey's kind and skilful conduct. He then thanked me for my attention to himself, and embracing me *à la Francaise*, said, "*Adieu Capitaine! comptez sur moi adieu!*" he seemed much affected.

In closing this narrative, I may be permitted to observe, that I endeavoured throughout, to execute the somewhat difficult mission with which I was charged, faithfully and zealously, but at the same time, with that deference and respect for the feelings of Napoleon, which appeared to me, no less due to his misfortunes, than to his exalted station and splendid talents.

Having shown in the foregoing conversation with Napoleon, his determination to have invaded England, had the force sent out to the West Indies eluded our fleet, it may not perhaps be considered uninteresting or irrelevant to state, to what circumstance was owing our escape from the misery, which would have been entailed on the country, had the enemy's fleet arrived in the channel.

No sooner had Nelson heard of Villeneuve's having sailed,

and conjecturing that his destination was the West Indies, than he lost no time in pursuing him, and though with only ten sail of the line, and his ships short of provisions, his decision was instantly made, and in the incredible short time of seventy days, arrived in the West Indies, watered at Barbados, visited all the islands, returned, watered again in Tetuan bay, and anchored at Gibraltar. Nelson was most singularly fortunate in the wind; he passed the combined squadron which was eight days sail ahead of him, short of provisions and water, he was obliged to run for Tetuan, where he anchored, the day Sir R. Calder fell in with the combined squadron.

He left Tetuan the 26th, passed the straits, and presented himself before Cadiz; not finding the enemy there, he went off Cape St. Vincent, cruised off the coast of Portugal, crossed the bay of Biscay, without meeting a single vessel that could give him any intelligence, and with indefatigable perseverance ran over to the coast of Ireland, and stopping, on the supposition of their going to Brest, he detached nine of his best ships to reinforce Admiral Cornwallis, and with the *Victory* and *Superb*, returned to Portsmouth. The arrival of the *Curieux* in England, with Nelson's despatches, acquainting the Admiralty of the return of the combined squadrons, was most fortunate; having had so much the start of Villeneuve, it gave the admiralty time to order the Rochfort squadron to unite with Sir R. Calder's squadron, off Terrol. This circumstance alone, baffled all Napoleons plans; he did not conceive it possible, that the government could be aware of Villeneuve's return; he thought a fleet having eighteen days start, could not possibly be outstripped by any single vessel. The *Curieux* left the West Indies, the 16th of June, and arrived the 11th of July.

Appendix

Discours de Napoleon a Sa Vieille Garde, a Fontainebleau, le 20 Avril, 1814.

Les Officiers, Soldats, et Tambours, rassemblés autour de lui (il les adressa ainsi) en présence des Officiers Autrichiens, Russes, Anglois, et Prusses, les Commissaires des Puissances Allieés—

Officiers, sous officiers et soldats de la Vieille Garde, Je vous fais mes adieu x. Pendant vingt ans Je vous ai toujours trouvés braves et fidèles, marchant dans le chemin de la gloire. L'ennemi en me dérobant trois marches, étoit entré dans Paris. Je marchois pour l'en chasser. Je vous remercie du noble élans que vous montrates dans cette place ci et ailleurs. Mais une partie de mon armée ne partageant pas vos sentimens m'abandonna, passa au camps ennemi. De ce moment la délivrance du capital devient impossible. J'aurois pu avec les trois quarts de l'armée qui me sont restéfideles et aidé des sentimens et des efforts de la grande majorité du peuple, porter mes pas sur la Loire ou dans plusieurs places, fortes et nourrir la guerre pendant plusieurs années. Mais les guerres étrangéres et civiles déchiroient le territoire de notre beau pays, et pour prix de tous ces sacrifices, et de tous ces ravages nous ne pourrions espérer de vaincre l'Europe réunie contre nous, ou la ville de Paris dont la plupart des habitans étoit sous l'influence d'une faction qui étoit parvenu à dominer. Toutes ces circonstances réunies, Je n'ai considéré que les interêts de la patrie, le repos de la France. J'ai fait le sacrifice de tous mes droits, Je suis prêt à faire celui de ma personne—le but de toute ma vie a été le bonheur et la gloire de la France. Quant à vous, soldats, soyez toujours fidelés dans le chemin du devoir et de l'honneur. Servez avec fidélite votre nouveau souverrain. La plus douce occupation de ma vie sera désormais de faire connôitre a la postérité ce que vous avez fait de grand et ma seule consolation sera d'apprendre ce que la France fera encore pour ajouter à la gloire de son nom. Vous êtes tous mes enfans. Je vous embrasse tous dans la personne de votre *Général, et en embrassant ces aigles qui nous ont servi de guides en tant de périls et de jours fortunés."* Lorsque Napoleon embrassa le Général Friant et les aigles, les larmes couloient des yeux de tous les vieux soldats. *"Adieu,"* (dit il) *"conservez moi dans votre souvenir.*

List Of Persons Accompanying The Emperor Napoleon To The Island Of Elba.

General Koeler, Comte Clam, (*Aide-de-Camp* to Prince Swartzenberg.) Austrian Envoys.
Colonel Campbell, English Envoy.
Comte Bertrand, Grand Marshal of the Palace.
Comte Druot, General of Division, and *aide-de-camp* to the Emperor.
Baron Germanowki, Major of the Light Horse Guards.
Chevalier Foureau, First Physician to the Emperor.
Chevalier Baillon, Chevalier Deschamps, Grooms of the Bedchamber.
Chevalier Perusse, Treasurer.
Mons. Gatte, Apothecary.
" Callin, Comptroller of the Household.
" Rothery, Secretary to the Grand Marshal.
" Gueval, Clerk to the Comptroller
" Pelard, Valet de Chambre.
" Hubert, Ditto.
" Sotain, Master of the Ceremonies.
" Purron, Officer of the Ceremonies.
" Rousset, Chief Cook.
" Lafosse, Chief Baker.

Mons Gaillard, Archambault, Paillett, Berthault, Villmaime, Valets.
" Dennis, Keeper of the Wardrobe.
" Gandron, Mathiers, Rousseau, Domestics.
" Armandran, Rider.
" Noverve, Body Servant.
" Besson, Renaud Grooms of the Stole.
" Chauvin, Sentini, Couriers.

H. M. S. *Undaunted*, off Antibes,
April 29th, 1814.

Sir—I have the honour to enclose for your information copies of letters I received from Colonel Campbell, commissioned by Lord Viscount Castlereagh, to accompany Napoleon to the island of Elba, likewise a copy of Sir Richard King's order. In compliance with Colonel Campbell's requisition, I embarked Napoleon at Frejus on the 28th inst.; he was accompanied by General Koller, Austrian Commissioner, and Comte Clam, *Aide-de-Camp* to Prince Swartzenburgh, with a numerous suite. The Russian Commissioner, Prince Schouwallof, and the Prussian Comte Truxos (who accompanied him to Frejus) returned to Paris that night.

I have the honour to remain, Sir,
Your most obedient
and faithful servant,
Thomas Ussher.
To Sir Edward Pellew, Bart,
Commander-in-Chief,
&c. &c. &c.

Caledonia, Genoa, 3rd May, 1814.

My Dear Sir—Your letters reached me by the *Merope* today only, and I fully approve of all you have done, in compliance with the request of Colonel Campbell, you will receive this by Locker, who I send over to receive any communications Colonel Campbell may have to confide to me. I need not desire you to assure the colonel of his having my entire confidence, as you know him so well. He will take an order for your proceeding to Frejus for Madame Pauline, and I am sure you have too liberal a mind not to do everything that is handsome by your enemies.

Take care to treasure up your anecdotes for us all, who are eager to devour.

When you have landed the lady, you may remain in that quarter or return to Genoa to me, and leave the *Rainbow* in charge, giving every caution that nothing unpleasant arises between him and

B———. But should any popular insurrection arise, I desire he will abstain from taking any part what- ever, but observe the strictest neutrality. He will, no doubt, be aided on such an event by the Colonel and Austrian Minister.

Believe me ever,
Faithfully yours,
Edward. Pellew.

P.S.—Locker will tell you that we heard overland of you and Napier being on shore at Marseilles, before your own report of opening that communication.

Extract of a Letter from Sir Edward Pellew, dated 16th May, on board the Caledonia, Genoa.

The desire of Colonel Campbell for a ship of war, appears to be for the purpose of keeping up his communication with Lord Castlereagh, and the respectability due to his situation, it is presumed, he will soon be directed to withdraw from Elba. Whenever the guards and followers of the Emperor are sent over, seven transports are employed to embark these objects at Savone whenever they arrive, when, probably, Elba will be left entirely to its Sovereign. I have received a letter from Lieutenant Smith, acting by your authority as Governor of the island of Capraja. I conclude long before this, that island is possessed by the Austrian troops, and that you have withdrawn that officer to his ship. I am very sorry to hear you have been unwell, and hope a little rest, which we shall all soon have, will restore you.

At the House of General Drenny,
Four, p.m.

Sir—I have the honour to acquaint you of my arrival here from Paris, with communications which regard the officer in command of his Britannic Majesty's ships on this station. Having been lately wounded, and much. fatigued, as well as from other circumstances, I trust you will excuse my not waiting on you, nor does the bearer know when I can have that honour. May I, therefore, request to see you as soon as convenient, in order that I may state to you the nature of my mission with which His Majesty's minister, Lord Viscount Castlereagh, has charged me.

I have the honour to be, Sir,
Your most obedient servant,
Neil Campbell, Colonel
Attached to the British Embassy at the
Court of St. Petersburg.

Marseilles, April 25th, 1814,
Eight, p.m.

Sir—I have the honour to acquaint you that Lord Viscount Castlereagh, His Majesty's principal Secretary of State for Foreign Affairs, has charged me with a mission, to accompany the late Chief of the French government, Napoleon Bonaparte, to the isle of Elba, to whose secure asylum in that island, it is the wish of His Royal Highness the Prince Regent to afford every facility and protection. Having, afterwards, written to his Lordship, that Napoleon had requested that a British ship of war might be given to him as a convoy to the French corvette, and at his option for embarkation, in case of preferring it, his Lordship wrote to me as follows, dated Paris, April 18th:—

> My instructions furnish you with authority to call upon His Majesty's officers, by sea and land, to give all due facility and assistance to the execution of the service with which you are entrusted. I cannot foresee that any enemy can molest the French corvette, on board of which, it is proposed, Napoleon shall proceed to his destination. If,

however, he shall continue to desire it, you are authorised to call upon any of His Majesty's cruisers (so far as the public service may not be thereby prejudiced) to see him safe to the island of Elba. You will not, however, suffer this arrangement to be made a cause of delay.

Napoleon has, since his departure from Fontainbleau towards St. Tropez, pressed me to proceed here for this object, which I beg leave to submit to your consideration, hoping, that as the desire to proceed immediately to his destination, as in unison with that of the Allied Powers, which would be defeated by delay; in referring to the Admiral commanding his Britannic Majesty's fleet, you will find yourself at liberty to proceed to St. Tropez with His Majesty's ship under your command.

I have the honour to be Sir,
Your most obedient servant,
Neil Campbell, Colonel
Attached to the Mission of H. E. General
Viscount Cathcart.
To Captain Ussher, senior officer of
His Britannic Majesty's ships,
off Marseilles.

Colonel Campbell informed me, that having been appointed by Lord Castlereagh to accompany Napoleon to the island of Elba, he arrived at Fontainebleau on the 16th, at nine in the morning; he met there Comte Bertrand, who expressed the Emperor's anxiety to proceed to his destination, and of his wish to change the place of embarkation from St. Tropez to Piombino. As there could be no certainty of his being received by the Commandant of Elba, and by going to Piombino that would be previously ascertained. If refused, he might be driven off the island by tempest while waiting permission to land. He expressed his hope that Colonel Campbell would remain at Elba until his affairs were settled, otherwise an Algerine corsair might land and do what he pleased. He seemed much satisfied when Colonel Campbell told him he had Lord Castlereagh's instructions to remain there for some time, if necessary, towards the security of Napoleon, in his communications by sea. After breakfast, Comte Flahaut informed the Commissioners that the Emperor would see them after he had attended Mass. The Commissioners were introduced in the following order:—Russian general Prince Schouwallof, who remained five minutes; Austrian general Baron Roller, the same time; Colonel Comte Truxos; Colonel Campbell, quarter of an hour, he asked him about his wounds and service, where his family resided, and seemed very affable.

Colonel Campbell received from Paris a copy of the order from General Dupont, Minister of War, to the Commandant at Elba, to give up the island to Napoleon, taking away the guns, stores, &c.

This displeased him exceedingly; he had a conversation with General Roller on the subject, and requested him to send his *aide-de-camp* with a note relating to it to Paris, wishing to know how he was to protect himself against any corsair, saying, if this conduct was continued he would go to England. A note was presented to the Commissioners by Comte Bertrand, who added verbally, that the Emperor would not disembark unless the guns were left for security and defence.

April 20th, the horses were ordered at nine a.m., he desired to see General Roller, he spoke warmly against the separation from his wife and child, also of the order for withdrawing the guns from Elba, saying, he had nothing to do with the Provisional Government, his treaty was with the Allied Sovereigns, and to them he looked for every act; he was not yet destitute of means to continue the war, but it was not his wish to do so. General Roller endeavoured to persuade him that the treaty would be fulfilled with honour. He then sent for Colonel Campbell, and resumed the conversation similar to what passed on the 17th, services, wounds, &c. the system and discipline of the British army, corporal punishments necessary, but to be applied seldom. He was much satisfied at Lord Castlereagh placing a British man-of-war at his disposal, if he wished it, for convoy or passage, complimented the nation. He then said he was ready;

the Duke of Bassano, General Belliard, Arnano, and four or five others his *aide-de-camps*, with about twenty other officers, were in the antechamber.

On entering the first room there was only General Belliard and Arnano, the *aide-de-camp* suddenly shut the door, so that it is presumed he was taking a particular leave of them; the door then opened, the *aide-de-camp* called out, The Emperor! he passed with a salute and smile, descended into the court, addressed his guards (see appendix) embraced General Petit and the colours, entered his carriage and drove off.

The 21st, slept at Brienne, in a large hotel, a good supper being provided; the Emperor supped with General Bertrand.

22nd, slept at Nevers, cries of "*Vive l'Empereur.*" In the morning he sent for Colonel Campbell, the table was laid, he desired the servant to lay another cover, and invited him to stay and breakfast. General Bertrand also joined them, He asked Colonel Campbell who commanded in the Mediterranean, he said, he did not know for certain, but believed Sir Sidney Smith was one of the admirals. When Comte Bertrand sat down, he said, laughing, "*que pensez vous, Sydney Smith, amiral dans la Mediterranée ;*" he then related his having thrown several thousand shot from his ships on shore without killing a man (this was at Acre.) It was his great source, for he paid so much for every shot brought in by the men, "*Il m'envoya les parliamentaires comme un second Marlborough.*"

The 23rd, before the journey this morning, he requested Colonel Campbell to go on, in order to expedite the British man of war, and also to write to Admiral Emeriau at Toulon, to expedite the French corvette; he sent off to Auxerre to order his heavy baggage, with the escort of six hundred guards and horses to go by land to Piombino; but if that was objected to, to go by Lyons and drop down the Rhone. Colonel Campbell proceeded on by Lyons and Aix, when he learned that I was at anchor in the bay of Marseilles, and where he arrived the following evening of the 25th.

The morning of the 20th, the Commissioners communicated to Comte Bertrand the facilities which had been obtained in regard to the several difficulties presented, respecting a director of posts for the horses, and British man-of-war for convoy or conveyance, and a copy of the order given by General Dupont. After the formation of the Provisional Government, a person was asked by Napoleon what he thought of his situation, and whether he thought there were any measures to be taken, he replied in the negative; he asked what he would do in a similar situation, he said, he would blow his brains out; he reflected a moment, "*Oui, je puis faire cela mais ceux qui me veulent du bien ne peuvent en profiter, et ceux qui me veulent du mal, cela leur feroit plaisir.*"

Frefus, April 27th, 1814,
Seven, a. m.

My Dear Sir—I have this moment arrived here, and observed your ship in the offing. As circumstances have rendered it necessary to change the place of Napoleon's embarkation from St. Tropez to Frejus, I despatch the bearer to announce it to you. I passed him on the road, so I do not know whether he means to wait for the corvette; but as I shall know in the course of the day, I shall lose no time in sending off to acquaint you, "in case you do not come on shore after you anchor." Napoleon will arrive here in an hour or two. As I have had no rest, I am just going to bed, and shall leave directions to let me know when you anchor, in order that I may be on the lookout for your coming on shore. That there may be no mistake, will you haul down the red flag on quitting your ship, and I shall have a person ready to observe it. My quarter is at Mr. Michel's Rue de St. Joseph. Information was sent to St. Tropez for you of the change.

Yours truly,
N. Campbell.

Copie Des Articles Du Traité De Paris, *Du 11 Avril*, 1814.

Art. 1.

Sa Majesté l'Empereur Napoleon renonce pour lui et ses successeurs et descendants, ainsi que pour chacun des membres de sa famille, a tout droit de Souveraineté, et domination, tant sur l'Empire Français, et le royaume d'Italie que sur tout autre pays.

Art. 2.

L. L. M. M. l'Empereur Napoleon et l'Imperatrice Marie Louise conserveront ces titres et qualitès, pour en jouir leur vie durant. La mère, les frères, soeurs, neveux et nièces de l'Empereur, conserveront egalement partout ou ils se trouveront ces titres de Princes de sa famille.

Art. 3.

L'Isle d'Elbe adoptée par S. M. l'Empereur Napoleon pour le lieu de son séjour formera sa vie durant, une principauté separée, qui sera possedée par lui, en toute sourveraineté et propriété. Il sera donné en outre en toute propriété a l'Empereur Napoleon, un revenu annuel de deux millions de francs, en rente sur le grand livre de France, dont un million reversible à l'Imperatrice.

Art. 4.

Toutes les Puissances Alliées, l'engageant a employer leurs bons offices, pour faire respecter par les barbaresques le pavilion, et le territoire de l'Ile d'Elbe, et pour que dans ses rapports avec les barbaresques, elle soit assimileé à la France.

Art. 5.

Les Duchés de Parme, Plaisance et Guastalla, seront donnés en toute propriété et souveraineté à S. M. l'Imperatrice Marie Louise. Ils *passeront à son fils, et à sa descendance en ligne directe. Le Prince son fils prendra dès ce moment le titre du Prince de Parme, Plaisance et Guastalla.*

Art. 6.

Il sera reservé dans les pays auxquels l'Empereur Napoleon renonce pour lui et sa famille, des domaines ou donne des rentes sur le grand livre de France, produisant un revenu annuel net, et deduction faite, de tout charge de deux millions, cinq cent mille francs, les domaines ou rentes appartiéndront en toute propriété, et pour en disposer comme bon semblera aux Princes et Princesses de sa famille, et séront repartés entre eux de manière à ce que le revenu de chacun, soit dans la proportion suivante savpir:—

	Francs.
A Madame Mère	*300,000*
Roi Joseph et la Reine	*500,000*
Roi Louis	*200,000*
Reine Hortense et ses enfans	*400,000*
Roi Jérome et la Reine	*500,000*
Princesse Elise	*300,000*
Princesse Pauline	*300,000*

Les Princes et Princesses de la famille de l'Empereur Napoleon consérveront en outre, tous les biens, meubles et immeubles, de quelque nature que ce soit, qu'ils possédent titre particulière, et notament les rentes dont ils jouissent (également comme particuliers) sur le grand livre de France, ou le monte Napoleone à Milan.

Art, 7.

Le traitement annuel de l'Imperatrice Josephine sera reduit à un million en domaines, ou en inscriptions sur le grand livre de France. Elle continuera à jouir en toute propriété de tous ces biens, meubles et immeubles particuliers, et pourra en disposér conformement aux loix Français.

Art. 8.

Il sera donné au Prince Eugene Vice Roi d'Italie, un etablissement convenable hors de France.

Art. 9.

Les propriétés S. M. l'Empereur Napoléon possèdeen France, soit comme domaines extraordinaires, soit comme domaines privés resteront à la Couronne, sur les fonds placés par l'Empereur Napoléon, soit sur le grand livre, soit sur la banque de France, soit sur les actions des forêts soit de toute autre manière, et dont S. M. fait l'abandon à la Couronne, il sera reservé un capital, qui n'excédra pas deux millions, pour être employés, en gratifications, en faveur des personnes, qui seront portiees sur l'Etat.

Art. 10.

Tons les diamans de la Couronne, resteront à la France.

Art. 11.

L'Empereur Napoléon fera retournér au tresor, et aux autres caisses publiques, toutes les sommes et tous les effets, qui en auraient été deplacés par ces ordres, á l'exception de ce qui appartient de la liste civile.

Art. 12.

Les dettes de la maison de S. M. l'Empereur Napoléon, telles qu'elles se trouvent au jour de la signature du present traité seront immediatement acquittés, sur les arrières dues par le trésor public á la liste civile, d'après les états qui seront signés par un Commissaire nommé a cet effet.

Art. 13.

Les obligations de Monte Napoleone de Milan, envers tous les Créanciers soit Français, soit étrangerés, seront exactement remplis, sans qu'il soit aucun changement à cet égard.

Art. 14.

On donnera tous les saufs conduits nécessaries pour le libre voyage de S. M. l'Empéreur Napoléon, et de l'Imperatrice, des Princes et Princesses, et de toutes les personnes de leur suite qui voudront les accompagner, ou s'établir hors de France, ainsi que pour le passage, de tous les équipages, chevaux et éffets qui leur appartiennent. Les Puissances Alliées, donneront en conséquence, des officiers et quelques hommes d'escorte.

Art. 15.

La Garde Impériale Français fournira un détachement de douze à quinze cents hommes tout armés, pour servir d'escorte jusqu'à St. Tropez lieu de 1'embarquement.

Art. 16.

Il sera fourni une corvette armée et les battiments de transport nécessaire pour conduire, au lieu de sa destination S. M. l'Empereur Napoléon ainsi que sa maison. La corvette démeurera en toute propriété á sa Majesté.

Art. 17.

Sa M. l'Emperéur Napoléon pourra emmenér avec lui et conserver pour sa garde quatre cents hommes de bonne volonté, tant officiers que sous officiers et soldats.

Art. 18.

Tous les Français qui auront suivé S. M. l'Empéreur Napoléon ou sa famille, seront tenus, s'ils ne veulent perdre leur qualite de Français, de rentrer en France, dans le térme de trois ans, à moins qu'ils ne soient compris dans les exceptions, que le gouvernement Français se reserve d'accordér après l'expiration de ce térme.

Art. 19.

Les troupes Polonaises de touts grades, qui sont au service de France, auront la liberté, de retourner chez elles, en conservant armes, et bagages, comme un temoinage de leurs services honorables. Les officiers, sous officiers et soldats, consérveront les decorations qui leur ont été accordéés, et les pensions attachés a ces décorations.

Art. 20.

Les hautes Puissances Alliées, garantissent l'execution de tous les articles du présent traité. Elles s'engagent à obtenir qu'ils soient adoptés et garantis par la France.

Art. 21.

Le présent traité sera ratifié, et les ratifications en seront échangés à Paris dans le terme de deux jours ou plutôt si faire se peut.

Fáit à Paris le onze Avril, mil huit cent quatorze.
Signé) Neselrode,
Secretaire de l'Empereur de la Russie.

Ney,
M'donald,
Berthier,
Maréchaux de l'Empire.

Pour copie conforme,
E. H. Locker.

From Elba To Paris,
By Colonel Laborde.

At Elba the Emperor lived much in the same way as he did in Paris. All strangers who were presented to him experienced a kind reception. After breakfast, he frequently took an airing in an open carriage, and almost always accompanied by General Bertrand. His favourite drive was about the neighbourhood of St. Martin, a place situated on the other side of the gulf. He dined at six o'clock, and in the evening received company, consisting of the residents of the island and their ladies, foreigners, officers, &c. The balls were very numerously attended. Princess Pauline, His Majesty's sister, did the honours at those entertainments, at which a vast throng of elegant ladies were always present.

During our abode on the island, the officers and sub-officers of the guard, together with several ladies, formed an amateur theatrical company. In the theatre attached to the Emperor's residence, several performances took place, at which His Majesty and all his household were present.

Subsequently, the Emperor built, at his own expense, a theatre at Porto Ferrajo. It was opened, during the carnival of 1815, with a grand masked ball, which commenced at six in the evening and ended at seven on the following morning. His Majesty and his suite were present at the ball, all attired in black dominos.

The Emperor frequently went to Porto Longo, which was about two miles distant from Porto Ferrajo. Colonel Germanoski, who was the military commandant of the former place, frequently gave brilliant balls, to which the officers of the

Imperial Guard and the ladies of Porto Ferrajo were invited. I often saw there the officers of an English ship, which was lying at anchor off Porto Longo.

Among the foreign ships which visited Elba, there were several belonging to the regencies of Algiers, Tunis, and Tripoli, It is impossible to describe the joy manifested by the crews of these ships whenever His Majesty honoured them with a visit. Their shouts of joy made the air resound. The captains said, that they regarded the Emperor as a God. These ships never departed without carrying with them proofs of the Emperor's generosity.

The Emperor behaved with marked liberality; he made several new roads which facilitated communication between various parts of the island. The inhabitants owe to him a debt of obligation which can never be forgotten.

It has been falsely stated, that several eminent individuals from France came to Elba, for the purpose of making arrangements with the Emperor for his return. Only one Frenchman, of any consequence, visited Elba; this was Henry de Chaboulon, formerly secretary to the Emperor, and his visit was but of short duration. During the nine months of our sojourn on the island no extraordinary circumstance occurred. We passed our time very gaily, amidst balls and other entertainments.

Every Sunday the Emperor attended mass, which was performed by Arrighi, the Vicar General of the island, in His Majesty's; all the civil and military authorities being present.

The preparations for our departure from the island were made with the greatest secrecy. On the morning of the 26th of February (the day of our embarkation) whilst walking on the promenade at the harbour, in company with Baron Galeuzzinio, the Civil Intendant of the island, I was informed that General Cambronne wished to see me at eleven o'clock in the forenoon. I waited upon him at the time appointed, and he directed me to go to General Druot to receive orders. The latter addressed me as follows:—

> The labourers who are employed in the gardens of the owners, leave off their work at three o'clock; at four, the

troops take their rations. You must then immediately pack up your arms and luggage, and hold yourself in readiness to embark at five o'clock. Each officer to take only a portmanteau.

These orders at first astounded me; but after a moment's pause, I ventured to ask General Druot where we were going, and whether I could take my wife with me?

"I cannot say," replied he, "obey the orders I have given you."

At five o'clock in the afternoon the troops embarked. Three hundred men and the staff battalion went on board the ship of war *Inconstant*; the rest of the troops were dispersed in different transport vessels. The Emperor after taking leave of Madame Mere and the Princess Pauline, with whom he had dined, repaired on board the *Inconstant* at eight o'clock in the evening, accompanied by Generals Bertrand, Druot, and Cambronne. We speedily set sail, and no one knew whither we were bound, until a trivial circumstance solved the riddle.

Lieutenant Taillade, an able officer, had commanded the brig *Inconstant* during our residence at Elba, but he had been superseded by Captain Chantard, who had arrived from the continent a few months previously. On the 28th of February, Lieutenant Taillade, who was perfectly acquainted with the navigation of the Mediterranean, observing that the new commander of the brig was steering towards a point opposite to the coast of France, said aloud to the officers on deck—"gentlemen, we are going either to Spain or Africa."

Colonel Mallet reported these words to the Emperor, who immediately sent for Taillade.

"Where are we?" said His Majesty, addressing that officer.

"Sire," answered Taillade, "we are steering towards Africa."

"I will not go there," said the Emperor, laughing, "Taillade," pursued he, "I confer on you the rank of captain. Take the command of the brig, and land me on the coast of France."

"Sire," said Taillade, "your Majesty shall be there tomorrow at noon."

The wind, which on the 27th had fallen almost to a calm, and left us off the island of Capraya, now rose to a strong breeze, and our new captain, in a few hours, brought us within sight of Antibes. At three o'clock, on the 1st of March, we landed in the gulf of Juan, between Caunes and Antibes.

The only incident worthy of remark that occurred whilst we were at sea, was our falling in with the French brig *Zephyr*, commanded by Lieutenant Andrieux, which frequently sailed to and fro between Toulon and Leghorn. On discovering the brig, the captain of the *Inconstant* intimated the circumstance to the Emperor, who immediately ordered that all the men on deck should lie flat down with their faces to the ground. Captain Taillade then took his speaking trumpet and called to Andrieux

"Whither are you bound, Commander?"

"To Leghorn. And you?"

"To Genoa."

"How is the great man?"

"Very well."

And the two brigs, after passing close alongside of each other, were soon far apart. The captain of the French brig little suspected that the great man was at that moment within hearing.

Before the vessel reached the landing place, the Emperor directed Captain Lamourette, commanding the first company of Chasseurs, to go ashore in a boat, accompanied by thirty men and one drummer. He was ordered to take possession of a fortification, which had been established a considerable time previously for the protection of the bay, and which His Majesty supposed was occupied by a detachment from the garrison of Antibes. Captain Lamourette found no one there; but urged by the desire of gaining partisans for the Emperor, and seeing the garrison manoeuvre on the glacis, he thought he had only to show himself and take possession of the fortress. Thither he accordingly marched. The sentinel advanced to meet him with the question "Who goes there?"

"The Emperor's guard," answered Captain Lamourette.

The sentinel presented arms and allowed the detachment to

pass; but the officer commanding the posts, when he perceived that the troops wore the tri-coloured cockade, ordered the draw-bridge to be raised, and the detachment of the guard was captured. The unfortunate detachment was conducted to Toulon, and there imprisoned in the casemates of Fort Lamalgue. The officers were tried by a court-martial, and would probably have been condemned to death, had not the authorities commanding at Toulon received tidings of the Emperor's arrival in Paris. The intrepid prisoners were then immediately liberated. They were then feasted and entertained, and paraded in triumph through the city. In the course of a few days the detachment arrived in Paris.

The disembarkation from the *Inconstant* was concluded at three o'clock on the afternoon of the 1st of March. I landed in the first boat, together with the worthy and respected General Drouot. There was a custom-house station in a wooden barrack near the spot where we landed, and its occupants, as soon as they descried us, hastily mounted the tri-coloured cockade.

His Majesty, having landed, ordered his bivouac to be established in an olive grove, between the gulf of Juan and the high road leading to Nizza, at a short distance from Carmes and the fortress of Antibes. As soon as the troops were landed, and before they could be posted in the proper stations requisite for covering His Majesty's bivouac, Lieutenant Sarri, a young naval officer of distinguished courage, received orders to sail with the whole flotilla to Corsica. This order was obeyed with such singular promptitude and activity, that a young orderly officer, belonging to a family of the island of Elba, who had fallen asleep in a corner of the vessel, was astonished, on awaking, to find the vessel several miles from the shore.

A few hours after the disembarkation, the staff physician, Emery, of the guard, whose family and numerous friends were in Grenoble, was ordered by the Emperor to proceed with the utmost haste to that city, and to seek out young Dumouline, who had visited the Emperor several times previous to our departure. His Majesty wished to make arrangements with him for printing the proclamations dated from the gulf of Juan, and getting them circulated in Grenoble and its neighbourhood.

The troops having been encamped round the Emperor's bivouac, General Cambroune, with a strong detachment, was despatched to Carmes with orders to collect as many horses as possible (paying for them a price beyond their value) and, at the same time, to guard the roads, and permit no travellers to pass. The general issued orders to the post masters prohibiting them from furnishing any one with horses without previous authorisation. A few hours after these orders were issued, a courier of the Prince of Monaco announced the approaching arrival of His Highness, and required to be furnished with a considerable number of horses; but General Cambroune decidedly refused permission for supplying them. In a short time the prince himself arrived, and earnestly solicited that the Emperor would permit him to continue his journey. His Majesty ordered that the prince should be allowed to proceed.

Captain Cazabianca, a native of Corsica, and a very meritorious officer, was sent by the Emperor to the Commandant of the fortress of Antibes; Colonel Cuneo (likewise a Corsican) with directions to liberate the detachment that had been captured; but Colonel Cuneo refused to obey the order, and even detained Captain Cazabianca. That brave officer, driven to despair by the thought of being prevented sharing the dangers of his companions in arms, made an attempt to escape by scaling the walls of the fortress. On the following day he was found lying in the moat, severely hurt. He was conveyed to the hospital of Antibes, where he remained for a considerable time. The commissary Banthier was next despatched; but he received warning not to approach the fortress. At last I was sent to the Commandant of Antibes; but scarcely had I reached the first outposts than he called to me—"Go back, or I will fire upon you." Finding it impossible to gain access to the fortress, I sent intimation of that fact to General Druot.

We left our bivouac about eleven o'clock at night. The Emperor, at the head of his handful of brave followers, marched in the direction of Grasse, which place we reached at eleven o'clock on the 2nd of March. The column halted and took up a position at the outskirts of the town, where the Emperor's breakfast was prepared. During the repast, His Majesty received several of the most distinguished residents of Grasse, among others, an officer decorated with the cross of honour; he had lost his sight, and was led in by his wife. The Emperor received him in the kindest manner imaginable. The officer begged permission to kiss His Majesty's hand: the Emperor embraced him.

Breakfast being ended, and the troops (who were supplied with provisions and various sorts of wine by the inhabitants) having had a little rest, we pursued our march, leaving our artillery behind; indeed, it would have been impossible to convey it along the steep and difficult roads we had to traverse. We had a most fatiguing day, threading our way through the narrow passes of Provence. We marched along paths which scarcely afforded sufficient width for one man, and which were surrounded by frightful abysses; in short, we were in such a position that fifty men might have checked our advance.

Our column, which consisted of between 1000 and 1100 men, extended over such a lengthened space, that it might have been taken for a column of 2,500 men. We marched the whole day amidst snow and ice. The Emperor was obliged to alight from his horse, and to go several miles on foot. He was so fatigued, that we found it necessary occasionally to support him by holding his arms, and he several times fell, after a march of many hours. Having advanced about twenty leagues on our way to Paris, we arrived at a solitary country house, not far from the village of Cernon.

There the Emperor passed the night, with such accommodation as the desert place was capable of affording. Our beds consisted of bundles of straw, and His Majesty rested as well there, perhaps better, than he had frequently reposed in the palace of the Tuilleries, though he was surrounded by only 500 men of his guard and a few officers. The rest of the column, which was scattered about, passed a miserable night, and all our force was not collected together until the following day, the 3rd of March, about midday. We then marched on Castellone. From thence we sent forward our baggage, and the column marched daily, in groups, in the direction of Grenoble. On the 3rd, the Emperor passed the night at Barcone, and on the 4th at Digne. On the 5th, General Cambroune, with the advanced guard of forty men, made himself master of the bridge and the fortress of Sisteron. The Emperor passed the night of the 5th at Gap, and the advanced guard was quartered at Mure.

During our march across the extent of country, no remarkable incident occurred. The inhabitants received us kindly, but without declaring for or against us. Throughout this long march we gained only two recruits, a *gen-d'arme* and a foot soldier. At length, to our great joy, we emerged from this mountainous district, and entered upon the smiling vicinity of the Mure, from thence to proceed to Grenoble.

The Emperor, being informed that the garrison of Grenoble had marched out with the intention of preventing him from crossing the bridge of the Mure, made his arrangements, dividing his small force, scarcely 1100 men, into three columns. The first, consisting of three companies of *chasseurs*, the Polish lancers, mounted and unmounted, and eight or ten men of the marine guard, formed the advanced guard, commanded by General Cambroune, assisted by the intrepid Colonel Mallet. The second column, commanded by Captain Loubers of the grenadiers, consisted of three companies of grenadiers, the artillery company, and about thirty officers without men, headed by the Corsican Major Pacconi; the Emperor, the whole of the staff, and the *caisse*, drawn by two mules, accompanied the second column. The third column, consisting of the Corsican battalion, commanded by the Chef de Battaillon Guaso, formed the rear guard.

As we approached the Mure, General Cambroune ordered me, accompanied by sixty *chasseurs*, commanded by Lieutenant Jeanmaire, and a few Polish lancers, to form the head, and to dispose our first column in such a position that I might seem to be followed by 1,200 men, though I had with me scarcely three hundred. It appeared that we were expected, for I found the whole municipal body assembled at the Mairie.

In a few moments General Cambroune came up with the first column. Perceiving an enemy's post, stationed in some houses on the road leading to Grenoble, the general posted a party of our troops, commanded by an officer, within pistol shot of them. He dispatched Captain Raoul of the artillery, accompanied by the quartermaster of the Mamelukes, to the officer commanding the post of the 5th Regiment, to request that he would treat with us; but he could not be prevailed on to do so. The general went to him himself; but he received for answer that all negotiation was forbidden.

General Cambroune immediately stationed his column on the place in front of the Mairie, and adopted the requisite measures for guarding against a surprise. These operations being completed, we proceeded to an inn, opposite to the Mairie, where I had ordered a dinner for twelve. No sooner had we sat down to table, than a peasant, who had been directed by General Cambroune to watch the enemy's troops, informed us that the column was beginning to move, apparently with the intention of retiring behind the Mure, blowing up the bridge over which we had passed, and thereby cutting us off from all communication with the Emperor. We immediately stationed ourselves on the bridge, of which we retained military possession throughout the night, whilst the enemy's force retired on Grenoble, three leagues distant.

General Cambroune sent to inform the Emperor of what was going on, and about nine o'clock on the following morning, his Majesty arrived at the point of which we were in possession, placed himself at the head of the troops, and directed General Cambroune where to march. The brave Colonel Mallet took the command of the companies of *chasseurs*, forming the head of the column, and the Polish lancers, commanded by the gallant Colonel Germanoski, covered the right side of the march. The officers, without commands, headed by Major Pacconi, covered our left, and we marched straight towards the battalion of the 5th Regiment of the line. The *voltigeur* company was stationed at the furthest extremity of the village. The Emperor commanded Colonel Mallet to advance with the musket on the left arm and the bayonet inverted, the point being in the mouth of the barrel. The colonel observed that to adopt such a step in the face of a force whose intentions were unknown, and whose first impulse might be hostile, was hazardous. The Emperor replied hastily— "Mallet, do as I order."

On arriving within pistol shot of the regiment, the Emperor exclaimed in a loud and firm tone of voice—"Soldiers, behold your Emperor, which of you will fire on him!"

A young officer, *aide-de-camp* to General Marchand, Commandant of Grenoble, and who had been instructed by his general to oppose our advance, gave the word of command "Fire."

He was answered by a unanimous shout of "*Vive l'Empereur.*"

No sooner had we made friends with the 5th Regiment, than Dumoulin appeared, wearing in his hat the tri-coloured cockade. He advanced to the Emperor, and alighting from his horse, he eagerly exclaimed "Sire, I come to offer you 100,000 men and my arm, and to assure you of the fidelity of your good people of Grenoble."

The Emperor seemed pleased, and smiling, said, "mount your horse, Dumoulin, and we can talk together on our march. I accept your offer."

On the evening of our arrival at Grenoble, the brave young Dumoulin was appointed one of the Emperor's orderly officers, and His Majesty invested him with the decoration of the Legion of Honour. During the whole of our march from Grenoble to Paris, Dumoulin, with a party of fifty hussars of the gallant 4th Regiment, formed our advance guard, and rendered the greatest service to the Emperor's cause.

Immediately after Dumoulin joined us, the troops were ranged in marching order. The *chasseurs* of the guard formed the advance guard, and I, accompanied by some pioneers and a party of Polish Lancers, marched at the head, in order to prepare for the entrance into Grenoble. We passed Vizilla without any remarkable occurrence. About four in the afternoon, a young sub-lieutenant of grenadiers of the 7th Regiment of the line, came up to me, and said, "Major, is the Emperor far off?"

"No," replied I, "only half a league: you will soon see him."

"My Colonel," continued the sub-lieutenant, "whom you will come up with in about twenty minutes, is impatiently waiting His Majesty at the head of his fine regiment."

Accordingly we soon joined the unfortunate Labedoyere at the head of his fine regiment. He advanced to meet me, and enquired whether the Emperor was far distant. I replied that he would be soon in sight. The joy manifested by the colonel, at this information, is indescribable. I continued my march to the gates of Grenoble, and had begun to think about entering the city, when the Emperor came up, accompanied by his staff and the Polish lancers. Without a moment's delay I turned to the gate, which opened to the suburb of the town, I found it closed, though it was only half-past six in the evening. I required that it should be opened. Captain Raoul, of the artillery, made the same demand, as did likewise the major of the 11th Infantry, who was with his regiment on the outside of the garrison.

The major, calling to the colonel of the 5th Regiment of the line, who had possession of the keys, said, "Open the gate, my good fellow, the Emperor is here." The colonel replied, " I dare not; I have pledged my word of honour to the prefect (Fourrier) and the general (March and) to prevent the Emperor's troops from entering the garrison." All my appeals were vain. It was not until near eight o'clock that the colonel determined to open the gate, and then only on being assured that the inhabitants of the suburb were preparing to force it open. The troops then immediately took possession of the ramparts, amidst shouts of "*Vive l'Empereur.*"

The inhabitants came out bearing torches, and the Emperor soon entered Grenoble at the head of his army.

On the 9th of March, the Emperor and his guard passed the

night at Bourgoing. From Grenoble to Lyons, his march resembled a triumphal procession. The 4th Regiment of Hussars, which was sent forward to reconnoitre Lyons, was received in the suburb Guilla-iere, at four o'clock in the afternoon of the 10th of March, with shouts of "*Vive l'Empereur.*" At eight in the evening His Majesty marched into the city, at the head of those same troops who had been destined to oppose his entrance. On the 11th he reviewed all the troops collected at Lyons, amounting to 25,000 men. General Brayer, leading the advanced guard, marched forward to the capital.

On the 13th of March, the Emperor, at the head of the guard and the 7th Regiment of the line, entered Villefranche, a small town, having a population of 4000 souls; but which, at that moment, contained upwards of 60,000. At a late hour, that same day, the Emperor reached Macon, the inhabitants of the neighbouring districts thronging round him, and giving vent to the most enthusiastic expressions of joy.

On the morning of the 14th we reached Tournus, and the Emperor, with the guard, passed the night at Autun. On the 16th, we were at Avallon. On the 17th, His Majesty breakfasted at Vermenton, and that night slept at Auxerre. There we were joined, at eleven o'clock at night, by the gallant Colonel Marin of the artillery of the guard, who had come from La Fere to welcome His Majesty. At Auxerre, too, we were joined by the troops of the Prince of the Moskowa.

On the 20th of March, the Emperor, with the guards and the 7th Regiment of the line, entered Fontainbleau, where he was agreeably surprised to find Poles stationed as *videttes* at the gates of the castle. This able forced march, truly worthy of Polish troops, was conducted by Colonel Germanoski, commander of the Poles at Elba. On the same day the Emperor set off for Paris, where he arrived about nine o'clock in the evening.

Thus ended this gigantic enterprise, undertaken with a column of 1000 men, and accomplished without shedding a drop of blood.

Napoleon's Last Voyage

Extract From a Diary of
Sir George Cockburn

Contents

Preface   81
Extract From a Diary   83

Preface

The M.S. from which this "Extract" has been printed, was found, in his own handwriting, among the papers of my late father; attached to it being a note, also in his own handwriting, to the effect that it is a reproduction of a copy found at St. Helena, in 1824 or 25, among the effects of one who had held an official position as Admiral's Secretary or Captain's Clerk on board the *Northumberland* on her voyage to St. Helena, where he died, and who had no doubt made it as a matter of pardonable curiosity and satisfaction for himself; and it is now published in the belief that it's intrinsic interest, as closing a gap in the later career of the great soldier, will be deemed sufficient excuse for its seeing the light.

Thos: Salkeld Borradaile.
Surbiton, 1888.

Extract From a Diary of Rear-Admiral Sir George Cockburn

WITH PARTICULAR REFERENCE TO GENERAL NAPOLEON BUONAPARTE, ON PASSAGE FROM ENGLAND TO ST. HELENA, IN 1815, ON BOARD H.M.S. NORTHUMBERLAND, BEARING THE REAR-ADMIRAL'S FLAG.

On the 6th August, being off the Start in the *Northumberland*, I met Lord Keith in the *Tonnant*, having with him the *Bellerophon* and some frigates in which were General Buonaparte and all his suite. As the removal of the general and his things was likely to occupy some time, and the doing of it with the ships under sail might be attended with inconvenience, Lord Keith agreed with me in the propriety of anchoring the whole off the Berry Head, which was accordingly done the same evening; and his lordship afterwards accompanied me on board the *Bellerophon* to make known to General Buonaparte that in pursuance of instructions under which I was acting, he, the general, was to be removed as quickly as convenient into the *Northumberland* for the purpose of being conveyed to St. Helena. The general protested very strongly against this proceeding and against the right of the British Government thus to dispose of him. Very little other conversation passed between us; we did not think it necessary to enter into the merits of the question with him, but contented ourselves with observing that, as military officers, we must, of course, obey the instructions of our Government, and therefore that we hoped he would be ready to remove to the *Northumberland* the next morning.

On the 7th August, after breakfast, I went again to the *Bellerophon* to examine the baggage, &c., of the general and of those who were to accompany him, at which he was extremely indignant. I, however, in conformity with my instructions, caused everything to be inspected previous to permitting it to be sent on board the *Northumberland*; all the arms of every description were delivered up by him and his suite, and I stopped 4,000 *napoleons* in gold, which I delivered to Captain Maitland to be by him transmitted to the Lords Commissioners of the Treasury. Everything else belonging to them being transhipped and the necessary arrangements completed, about midday Buonaparte embarked on board the *Northumberland*, with the persons under mentioned, *viz.*

Grand Maréchal Comte de Bertrand.
Madame de Bertrand.
3 children of *ditto,*
1 female servant with her child,
1 man servant.

General Comte de Montholon.
Madame de Montholon.
1 child.
1 female servant.
Le Comte de Las Cases.
1 son (a boy about 13 years of age).

General Gourgaud.
3 *valets de chambre.*
3 *ditto de pied,*
1 *maitre d'hôtel.*
1 *chef d'office.*
1 cook,
1 *huissier.*
1 *lampiste.*

Of which—
7 grown-up, to be at my table.
2 maid servants, 1 young gentleman 5 children at a separate table.
12 domestics, with my servants.
27 in all.

On reaching the deck he said to me, "Here I am, Admiral, at your orders!" He then asked to be introduced to the captain, then asked the names of the different officers and gentlemen upon deck, asked them in what countries they were born and other questions of such trifling import, and he then went into the cabin with Lord Keith and myself, followed by some of his own people. After I had shown him the cabin I had appropriated for his exclusive use and requested him to sit down in the great cabin, he begged me to cause the lieutenant of the ship to be introduced to him; as, however, at this time his own followers came to take leave of him, I thought it best to leave him for a little while to himself, and I found soon afterwards advantage was taken of this for him to assume exclusive right to the after, or great cabin.

When I therefore had finished my letters I went into it again with some of my officers and desired M. de Bertrand to explain to him that the after cabin must be considered as common to us all, and that the sleeping cabin I had appropriated to him could alone be considered as exclusively his. He received this intimation with submission and good humour and soon afterwards went on deck, where he chatted loosely and good-naturedly with everybody.

At dinner he ate heartily of almost every dish, praised everything and seemed most perfectly contented and reconciled to his fate. He talked with me during dinner much on his Russian Campaign, said he meant only to have refreshed his troops at Moscow for four or five days and then to have marched for Petersburg, but the destruction of Moscow subverted all his projects, and he said nothing could have been more horrible than was that campaign; that for several days together it appeared to him as if he were marching through a sea of fire owing to the constant succession of villages in flames which arose in every direction as far as his eye could reach; that this had been by some attributed to his troops but that it was always done by the natives. Many of his soldiers however, he said, lost their lives by endeavouring to pillage in the midst of the flames.

He spoke much of the cold during their disastrous retreat, and stated that one night, after he had quitted the army to return to Paris, an entire half of his Guard were frozen to death. He also told me in the course of this evening that previous to his going to Elba he had made preparations for having a navy of 100 sail of the line; that he had established a conscription for the navy, and that the Toulon Fleet was entirely manned and brought forward by people of this description; that he ordered them positively to get under weigh and manoeuvre every day the weather would permit of it, and to stand out occasionally and to exchange long shots with our ships; that this had been much remonstrated against by those about him and had cost him at first a good deal of money to repair the accidents that occurred from the want of maritime knowledge, such as from the ships getting aboard of each other, splitting their sails, springing their masts, &c., but he found that even these accidents tended to improve the crews and therefore he continued to pay his money and oblige them to continue to exercise.

He said he had built his ships at Antwerp in rather too great a hurry, but he spoke highly in praise of the port and said he had already given orders for a similar establishment to have been formed on the Elbe; and had fortune not turned against him he hoped to have sooner or later given us some trouble, even on the seas. He stated that the reason he had over-hurried the ships at Antwerp, before mentioned, was because he was anxious to press forward an expedition from thence against Ireland. After taking his wine and coffee he took a short walk on deck and afterwards proposed a round game at cards; in compliance with which we played at *vingt-un* until about half-past ten, won from him about seven or eight *napoleons*, and he then retired to his bedroom, apparently as much at his ease as if he had belonged to the ship all his life. I afterwards disposed of his whole party for the night, though not without some difficulty; the ladies with their families making it necessary I should provide them with adequate room and accommodation, and yet each other person of the suite asking for and expecting a separate cabin to sleep in and in which to put their things.

On the 8th August, we lay-to the most of the day off Plymouth, waiting to be joined by the squadron destined to accompany us. It had blown fresh during the night, which left rather a heavy swell, the effect of which prevented General Buonaparte from preparing for dinner (at least that was the excuse made for his non-appearance), and I consequently did not see him during the day.

On the 9th August, being joined by all our squadron (except the *Weymouth* which I could not wait for), we proceeded on our way down Channel, with tolerably fine weather but wind from N.W. General Buonaparte came out of his cabin, for the first time this day, about two p.m. and took a short walk on deck, but as I was busy writing I did not see him until dinner time. I found him rather lower and more reserved than the first day; indeed, until after drinking a tumbler of champagne he hardly spoke at all, but afterwards he conversed with more freedom, and made many and particular enquiries on the number and state of our forces in India; said he had been in correspondence with Tippoo Saib, and that he had hoped to have reached India when he went to Egypt, but the removal of the *Vizier*, and the alteration of politics of the Ottoman Porte, with other circumstances, had prevented his pursuing the career there which he had at first contemplated. After dinner he went upon deck, and persisted in keeping off his hat as he walked up and down, evidently with a view to inducing the English officers on deck also to continue uncovered (as his French attendants did, and as I am told the officers of the *Bellerophon* used to do whilst he remained on the deck of that ship). Observing this, I made a point of putting on my hat immediately after the first compliment upon going out, and I desired the officers to do the same, at which he seemed considerably piqued, and he soon afterwards went into the cabin and made up his party at *vingt-un*, but he certainly neither played nor talked with the same cheerfulness he did the first night: this might, indeed, have been accident, but it appeared to me to proceed rather from downright sulkiness, though I cannot but remark that his general manners, as far as I am yet able to speak of them, are uncouth and disagreeable, and to his French friends most overbearing if not absolutely rude. About eleven he retired to his bedroom, having been as unfortunate at his *vingt-un* party as the evening before. (Just before dark this evening I dispatched a brig to put letters into the Post Office at Falmouth, off which place we were, to inform Government of our progress.)

On the 10th August, as soon as the brig I had sent to Falmouth rejoined me, we made sail on the starboard tack, the wind being still from the westward with considerable swell from that quarter. Buonaparte did not make his appearance until just before dinner, when I found him playing at chess in the great cabin with the Comte de Montholon. He appeared to me to play but badly, and was evidently inferior to his antagonist, who I observed nevertheless was quite determined not to win the game from His Ex-Majesty.

At dinner, Buonaparte told me, when talking about our late contests with America, that Mr. Maddison was too late in declaring his war, and that he never made any requisition to France for assistance; but that he (Buonaparte) would very readily have lent any number of line-of-battle ships Mr. Maddison might have wished for, if American seamen could have been sent to man them and carry them over; but that the affairs of France beginning to go wrong about that period, it was out of his power to afford any other material assistance to the American Government.

Immediately after dinner today, the general got up rather uncivilly and went upon deck as soon as he had swallowed his own coffee and before all the rest of us were even served. This induced me to request particularly the remainder of the party to sit still, and he consequently went out only attended by his *maréchal*, without the slightest further notice being taken of him. (It is clear he is still inclined to act the Sovereign occasionally, but I cannot allow it, and the sooner therefore he becomes convinced it is not to be admitted the better.)

General Gourgaud (who was in the Battle of Waterloo) told me today that during that battle, when the Prussians appeared, Buonaparte believed them to have been General Grouchy's Division, he having left between 30,000 and 40,000 men with that general, under orders to advance (in the same direction from which the Prussians had come) if from the firing heard General Grouchy should have reason to suppose the day was obstinately contested by the English; and this, he said, induced Buonaparte to persist in his efforts so long, and occasioned (when it was discovered that there were nothing but Prussians on the French flank) so general and complete a rout.

He said Buonaparte was forced off the ground at last by Soult, and he proceeded afterwards as quickly as possible to Paris; but so great was the panic and disorder among the French soldiers, that many of them (without arms or accoutrements) actually arrived in Paris (some behind carriages, others in carts, &c.), on the same day with the general and his attendants, not having halted once from the moment of their quitting the field, and reporting everywhere as they passed that all was lost. So well do these soldiers seem to have followed their chief's example in the hour of difficulty and danger!!!

Our latitude this day at noon was 49 41' N.

On the 11th August, it blew very fresh all day from the N.W., and I was forced to carry sail to weather Ushant, which occasioned all my French party, from the master to the man, to be miserably sick; I therefore saw nothing of General Buonaparte throughout the day. I had, however, some conversation with M. de Bertrand, which tended to prove to me how blindly attached he is to Buonaparte, and how decidedly inimical to the Bourbon family. He affirmed that neither Ney, nor Soult, nor any of the French *maréchals* were apprised of Buonaparte's intention of returning from Elba to France; that it was adopted by the general of his own accord, in consequence of his observing in the public papers how unwisely the Bourbons were acting, and which rendered him certain how unpopular they would be throughout France, and consequently that he (General Buonaparte) had only to shew himself there to be joined by everybody; but to the moment of his actually landing in France, he had not received a promise or a line from anybody with proposals or recommending the step. M. de Bertrand told me they landed with only 600 men; that he was sure Ney left Paris with the intention of obeying the king's orders and opposing Buonaparte's progress; but finding the soldiers he commanded, and indeed almost all his officers, resolved on joining Buonaparte instead of acting against him, he (Ney) then determined on taking the same line, as the only way of keeping the command of his division; and after having so resolved, he thenceforth acted most zealously for the new cause he had adopted, and did everything in his power to forward Buonaparte's views, and thwart and destroy those of the Bourbons.

Bertrand then added that General Buonaparte was received everywhere, as he advanced in France, like a father returning to his children, and that he would be always so received again in the event of his landing there (after the allied troops had quitted the country) owing to the love and affection borne him by every individual in the country. I could not help smiling at this statement of M. de Bertrand's, and asking him, in reply, if Buonaparte were so popular with all descriptions of persons throughout France, why he had so quickly determined on quitting it altogether after the defeat of Waterloo, instead of endeavouring to rally the dispersed armies, and make further efforts to defend the country? The only answer I could get from him to this question was, that General Buonaparte had expected to have been very differently received by the English; and that he had been much influenced in taking the step he had done by the Abbé Sieyes, who had strongly advised the General to proceed at once to England in preference to taking any other course.

Our latitude and longitude this day at noon were 48 48' N., 5 58' W.

On the 12th August our weather was more moderate, though the west wind and swell continued. Buonaparte came upon deck this day earlier than usual, that is to say about three o'clock. He does not generally quit his bed till between ten and eleven, and, like most Frenchmen, he breakfasts, reads, &c., before he makes his toilet, but he does not come out of his own cabin until he is dressed. He appeared today thoughtful and low, though in good health. I had a tolerably long conversation with him relative to Ferdinand of Spain: he said he considered him to be both a fool and a coward; that he was now perfectly under the dominion of the priesthood and was merely a passive instrument in the hands of the monks; he added, he looked upon King Charles of Spain as an honest good man, but that he had lost everything by his attachment to a bad wife.

He told me that Baron de Kolly, who was sent by our Government to bring off Ferdinand, was first found out by his endeavouring to gain some person to his interest in Paris, as also from suspicion excited by the command of money which he appeared to possess; that upon his being arrested all his papers were discovered, and then that it was determined to send off a police officer from Paris to personate Kolly at Vallancay, to deliver the Prince Regent's letter, and to assure Ferdinand that everything was prepared for his escape, purposely to prove how he would act under such circumstances; but in spite of everything this sham Kolly could urge (and Buonaparte added that he was a clever fellow) Ferdinand's courage was not equal to the undertaking, and he obstinately refused to have anything to do with the supposed agent of Great Britain. The general assured me that until Kolly was discovered at Paris the French Government had no idea of our attempting to carry off Ferdinand, but, however, that he was quite convinced, had Kolly not been discovered, that the pusillanimity of Ferdinand would have prevented all possibility of our success. I told him we had some suspicion of Baron de Kolly having played a double part in the transaction, but he said upon his honour it was no such thing.

Speaking of Captain Wright, he said that when Lord Ebrington, at Elba, first drew his attention to the name and to the circumstances respecting Captain Wright he did not recollect the case, which, he said, was exactly this; that Captain Wright, being supposed in France to have been concerned with the conspiracy of Georges and others, was, when taken, conveyed to the Temple preparatory to being examined with reference to that transaction, and on being ordered to attend a council charged with the investigation of it, he had put an end to himself. Buonaparte, though he confessed he could not give any reason for Captain Wright committing such an act, yet added that the inferior rank and little consequence of this officer ought to have exempted him (Buonaparte) from the charge of having either ordered or attached any importance to his death.

He asked me during this day's conversation a good many questions respecting the Spanish-American Colonies, and said he thought Spain would, by the present bigoted misconduct of Ferdinand, infallibly lose them all.

In the evening he played at *vingt-un* as usual until about eleven, but he did not seem to recover his spirits; he talked but little and appeared much absorbed in thought.

This day at noon we were in latitude 46 30' N., longitude 8 2' W.

On the 13th August, it was calm most of the twenty-four hours, but still we were attended by a disagreeable swell. I did not see much of General Buonaparte throughout this day, as owing to his appearing inclined to try to assume again improper consequence, I was purposely more than usually distant with him, and therefore, though we exchanged common salutations and high looks, nothing passed between us worth noticing.

Our latitude and longitude today at noon were 45 42' N., and 8 10' W.

On the 14th August, we had a continuation of fine weather and light winds. The general and myself were again distant and high with each other, though perfectly civil at least he has been as much so as his nature (which is not very polished) seems capable of and his attendants are certainly behaving as if anxious to gain my good opinion.

Our latitude and longitude today at noon were 45 13' N., 9 5' W.

On the 15th August, we had still light winds and fine weather with less swell than usual, which may in some measure account for General Buonaparte being more sociable and apparently more at his ease. It being his birthday I made him my compliments upon it and drank his health, which civility he seemed to appreciate; and after dinner I walked with him on deck and had rather a long conversation with him, in which I asked him whether he really had intended to invade England when he made the demonstration at Boulogne. He told me he had most perfectly and decidedly made up his mind to it, but his putting guns into the *praams*, and the rest of his armed flotilla, was only to deceive and endeavour to make us believe he intended to attempt making a descent on England with their assistance only, whereas he had never intended to make any other use of them than as transports; and he had entirely depended on his fleets deceiving ours by the routes and manoeuvres he directed them to make, and that they would thereby have been enabled to get off Boulogne, so as to have a decided superiority in the Channel long enough to ensure his making good his landing; for which he said everything was so arranged and prepared that he would only have required twenty-four hours after arriving at the spot fixed upon.

He said he had 200,000 men for this service, out of which 6,000 cavalry would have been landed with horses and every appointment complete, fit for acting the moment they were thrown on shore; that his *praams* were particularly intended for the carrying over these horses. He told me the exact point of debarkation had not been fixed upon by him, as he considered it not material and only therefore to be determined by the winds and circumstances of the moment; but that he had intended to have got as near to Chatham as he conveniently could, to have secured our resources there at once, and to have pushed on to London by that road. He said he had ordered his Mediterranean Admiral to proceed with his fleet to Martinique to distract our attention and draw our fleets after him, and then to exert his utmost efforts to get quickly back to Europe; and, looking into Brest (where he had ordered another fleet under Gantheaume to be ready to join him), the whole was to push up Channel to Boulogne, where Buonaparte was to be ready to join them and to move with them over to our coast at an hour's notice; and in point of fact, he said, he was so ready, his things embarked and himself anxiously looking for the arrival of his fleets, when he heard of their having indeed returned to Europe, but that instead of coming into the Channel in conformity with the instructions he had given, they had got to Cadiz, where they were blockaded by the English fleet, with which they had a partial engagement off Ferrol; and thus, he said, by disobedience and want of management of his admiral, he saw in a moment that all his hopes with regard to invading England were frustrated, with this additional disadvantage (which he had fully foreseen when he first turned in his mind the idea of such attempt), that the preparations at Boulogne had given a stronger military bias to every individual in England, and enabled ministers to make greater efforts than they otherwise perhaps would have been permitted to do.

He added that he believed, however, the English administration had entertained great alarms for the issue if he had got over, as his secret agents at the Russian Government reported to him that Great Britain had most pressingly urged that Court, with Austria, to declare war against France for the purpose of averting from England the danger of this threatened invasion; which he said, however, he had given up from the moment he found his fleets had failed him, and, having then turned his whole attention to his new enemies on the Continent, his forces collected at Boulogne enabled him to make the sudden movement which proved fatal to General Mac, and gave him (Buonaparte) all the advantages which followed. In short, the account he gave me very much tallied with Goldsmith's relation of the same circumstances (as given in his secret History of St. Cloud), and I must say, from what I have hitherto seen and learned, I begin to think Mr. Goldsmith had more foundation for many of his statements than he has generally received credit for. Buonaparte, however, told me in a manner not at all suspicious that Admiral Villeneuve decidedly put himself to death, though the general, in talking to me of him, seemed very strongly impressed with an idea of the admiral's unpardonable disobedience and misconduct throughout. He also told me that he had ordered Admiral Dumanois to be tried by a court martial for his conduct at the Battle of Trafalgar, and that he had exerted all his influence to get him shot or broke, but that he had been acquitted, in spite of him; and he added, when the sentence of acquittal was given, Admiral Cosmas (who was one of the Members of the Court, and who he said he decidedly considered to be the best sea officer now in France, and who has therefore been lately created a peer) broke his own sword at the time that of Dumanois was returned to him; which act Buonaparte seemed to have been most highly pleased with, and which was most probably the real cause of Cosmas's advancement to the peerage.

In the course of this evening's conversation he informed me that he had prepared a strong expedition at Antwerp, destined to act against Ireland, which he had only been prevented from sending forward by his own affairs beginning to take an unfavourable turn on the Continent.

His spirits throughout this day appeared considerably better than for some days past; he won a good deal at *vingt-un*, and his good fortune seemed to gratify him, the more as it was his birthday. He did not go to his bedroom this evening until past eleven o'clock.

Our latitude and longitude this day at noon were 43 51' N., and 10 21' W.

On 16th August, we had a continuation of fine weather, but light winds with calms. General Buonaparte is, I am glad to observe, evidently improving in his spirits and his behaviour, and as I am always ready to meet him half-way, when he appears to conduct himself with due modesty and consideration of his present situation, after dinner today I had a good deal of pleasant conversation with him; in the course of which some of the most remarkable circumstances he mentioned were, he assured me upon his word and honour (as Comte de Bertrand had done before), that he had not any communication or invitation from any of the *maréchals* or generals, or from any other person in France, when he returned to it from Elba, but that the public papers conveyed to him such an account of the state of France as induced him no longer to hesitate in taking the step he did: that on his getting within about five leagues of Grenoble, soon after his landing in France, a detachment of troops of the 3rd Regiment showed inclination to resist him; that he put himself immediately in front, and throwing open his great coat to shew himself more conspicuously, called to them to kill their Emperor if they wished it; that this had the effect he expected, and they all immediately joined him; and afterwards he received nothing but congratulations and proofs of attachment all the way to Paris.

He said, at Paris he had paid too much attention to and submitted too much to the opinion of the Jacobin party, which he now was persuaded had not been so requisite for him as he had conceived it to be, and that he should have done better if he had taken his measures from himself, and depended on his own popularity. He said the conduct of the allies obliged him to form his army, and move it, so quickly that he had not time to examine it and weed it as he should have done, and therefore many officers remained in it who had received their appointments from the Bourbons, and were extremely disaffected to him and anxious for opportunity to betray him. He said that he did not lose any soldiers from desertion on his march, but that his officers were constantly deserting. He then paid a compliment to the lower order of people in France at the expense of the higher orders. He said the former were the most sincere, the most firm, and at the same time the best dispositioned people in the world; but in proportion as you rose in class of people in France, the character became worse, and above the bourgeois they were too fickle and too volatile to be at all depended upon; they had one principle for today, and another for tomorrow, according to the circumstances of the moment; and he attributed solely to the disaffected officers of his army his Waterloo disasters.

He contradicted what General Gourgaud said the other day respecting his having mistaken the Prussians for General Grouchy's division, and assured me he knew early in the day the Prussians were closing on his flank; that this, however, gave him little or no uneasiness as he depended on General Grouchy also closing with him at the same time, and he had ordered a sufficient force to oppose the Prussians, who were in fact already checked; and he added that he considered the battle to have been upon the whole rather in his favour than otherwise throughout the day, but that after dusk the disaffected officers he had alluded to promulgated the cry of "*sauve qui peut*," which spread such confusion and alarm throughout his whole line, that it became impossible to counteract it, or to rally his troops, situated as they were; though he said had it been daylight, he was positive the result would have been different, as he then would only have had to have placed himself in a conspicuous situation in the front to have insured the rallying of all his troops around him, but, as it was, treachery and darkness combined rendered his ruin inevitable.

He said he did not on the morning of the 18th June entertain the most distant idea that the Duke of Wellington would have willingly allowed him to have brought the English army to a decisive battle, and he (Buonaparte) had therefore been the more anxious to push on, and if possible force it, as he considered nothing else could offer him a chance of surmounting the difficulties with which he was surrounded; but, he added, if he could have beaten the English army, which (from the approximation of their numbers) he was led to consider possible, the situation was such that he was positive hardly any of the English forces would have escaped being either killed or taken; that the Russian army, having been already beaten on the 16th, would (upon any decided disaster to the English) have been forced to make a precipitate retreat and perhaps have been dispersed, certainly entirely disorganized; that he (Buonaparte) might then have pushed by forced marches to have met the Austrians before any junction could have taken place between them and the Russians, which would have placed the game in his hands even if hostilities had been obstinately persevered in; though, in the then state of things, he had built, he said, rather upon the idea that a victory over the English army in Belgium, with its immediate results, would have been sufficient to have produced a change in the Administration in England and have afforded him a chance of concluding an immediate general truce; which was really his first object, as France was hardly equal to the effort she was then making, and it was perfectly impossible for her to think of making any adequate resistance against the numerous forces of the Allies if once united and acting in concert against him.

He said things, however, having taken the turn they did, and forced him, consequently, to act as he had done, he thought Great Britain had not pursued the wisest policy in refusing to receive him in a friendly manner; that he would have given his word of honour not to have quitted the kingdom nor to have interfered in any manner, directly or indirectly, in the affairs of France or in politics of any sort, unless hereafter requested so to do by our Government; that the influence he had over the minds of people of every description in France would have enabled him to have kept them quiet under whatever terms it might have been thought necessary for the future security to impose upon France; but that if terms at all repugnant to the vanity of the French nation are acquiesced in by the Bourbons it will render them, if possible, even more unpopular than they now are, and the people of France will only await a favourable crisis to rise *en masse* for their destruction. He said the disbanding of the French army was of no great consequence, as the whole nation was now military and could always form into an army at a given signal.

In answer to all this I told him very fairly that, conscious as he no doubt was of his own integrity and how sacredly he would have observed any stipulations to which he pledged his word of honour, it was, perhaps, natural for him at the moment to feel as he had stated; yet that I did not think, after the events of latter years, the Government of Great Britain could be supposed to have sufficient reliance on him to have allowed him to take up his abode in England in conformity with his request, due reference being had to the present state of things in France and to the feelings of our allies on the Continent; and I therefore observed to him, that, with this view of the subject, I had been surprised at his not retiring in preference to Austria, where his connection with the Emperor would have afforded him so strong a claim to more distinguished reception and consideration. He said if he had gone there he had no doubt he would have been received with every attention, but that he could not bring himself to receive any favours from the Emperor of Austria after the manner in which he had now taken part against him, notwithstanding his former professions of affection and his close connection with him; which latter, the general added, had not been by any means sought by himself

He then gave me the following curious relation respecting his marriage with Maria Louisa. He told me that when he was with the Emperor of Russia at Erfurth, Alexander took an opportunity of pressing upon him one day how important his having a legitimate heir must prove to the repose of France and Europe; and Alexander therefore advised his setting aside Josephine, to which, if he would consent, the Emperor offered him in marriage a Russian princess (Buonaparte said he believed the Emperor called her the Princess Ann); but he said he did not pay much attention to it at the time, for he had lived so long in such harmony, and had so much reason to be satisfied, with Josephine, that the idea of causing her pain disinclined him from then entering further on the subject; added to which, he said, he was already well aware of the falseness of character of the Emperor Alexander. He therefore merely observed to him in reply, that he was living on the best terms possible with the Empress

Josephine, and consequently had never turned his thoughts towards any arrangement of the nature mentioned by his Imperial Majesty. However, some time afterwards at Paris, being strongly pressed by his friends on the same point, and Josephine having herself assented to the arrangement, he sent to Russia to acquaint Alexander with his wish and readiness to espouse the Russian princess who had been proffered to him.

This intimation, he said, the Russian government received with every outward mark of satisfaction, professing its readiness to accede to the match, but at the same time starting difficulties upon various points connected with it, and particularly with regard to securing to the princess the right of exercising her own religion, to which end it was demanded a Greek chapel might be established for her in the Tuilleries. This, Buonaparte said he would not have cared about himself, but being a thing so uncustomary, it, with the other points requested by Russia, caused much discussion and difficulty at Paris; therefore, in consequence of these inconveniences presenting themselves with regard to the Russian alliance, some of his ministers, with Eugene Beauharnois (his son-in-law), waited upon him to press the advantage it would be if he would consent to ask in marriage an Austrian princess instead, adding that the Austrian Ambassador would readily engage for his court coming into any arrangements he (Buonaparte) might wish for this object; to which he replied if such were the case, and the thing could be concluded at once, he should not on his part make objections to this new plan.

It was, therefore, almost immediately agreed upon to take the contract of marriage of Louis XVI. for their guide in arranging his with an Austrian princess, and before twelve o'clock that night the necessary documents were prepared and signed and sent off for the approbation of the Emperor of Austria; who acceded without hesitation to everything, and by his manner of forwarding it, gave all reason to believe that he was not only satisfied, but highly pleased with the arrangement; and thus Buonaparte said he became the Emperor's son-in-law without any other solicitation or intrigue on his part, and without having even once seen Maria Louisa until she arrived in France as his wife. He therefore seemed to think that the Emperor's conduct towards him, since his reverses began, was not in unison with his conduct or professions towards him in prosperity, or such as he had a right to expect from the father of his wife; and consequently he said he would rather have gone anywhere in his distress, or done anything, than have placed himself in a situation to have been obliged to ask protection as a favour from a prince who he thought had behaved towards him so unjustly.

He finished by saying he had been deceived with respect to the reception he looked for from the English, but still, harshly and unfairly as he considered himself treated by them, yet he found comfort from feeling that he was under the protection of British laws; which he could not have felt had he gone to any other country, where his fate might have depended on the whim of an individual. He hardly said anything more about his wish to have gone to America, and though his attendants assured me he was very anxious to have got there, and to have remained there as a private individual, I believe he gave up all idea of that country after the passports were refused him, and he saw the situation of our ships. He played his game of *vingt-un* this evening as usual, and went to bed about ten o'clock.

Our latitude and longitude were today at noon 42 59' N., and 10 42'W.

On the 17th August we had light baffling weather. In my conversation this day with General Buonaparte, the only thing which passed, worthy of noticing, was his remarking to me, amongst other things, that he had been placed in chief command as a general officer at the age of twenty-four years; that he made the conquest of Italy at twenty-five; that he had risen from nothing to be sovereign of his country (as Consul) at thirty; and that if chance had caused him to have died or to have been killed the day after he entered Moscow, his would have been a career of advancement and uninterrupted success without a parallel; and the very misfortunes which afterwards befell the

French army would in such case probably have tended rather to the advantage than disadvantage of his fame, as, however inevitable they were, they would certainly have been attributed to his loss rather than to their true cause.

The general left the *vingt-un* party rather abruptly this evening and retired earlier than usual.

Our latitude and longitude this day were 41 57' N., 11 n'W.

On the 18th August we had fine weather with light winds from the westward. The brig I sent to Guernsey joined us again this day, which enabled me to give General Buonaparte some French papers and gazettes which she brought. He told me in the evening that the *Presidents des Departements* and *des Arrondissements* appointed by the king were, with very few exceptions, the same persons as he (Buonaparte) should have appointed. In the course of our conversation this evening he talked much of the late Queen of Naples and said he had had a good deal of correspondence with her, as well whilst he was in Sicily as in Naples: he said his general advice to her was to remain quiet and not to intermeddle with the arrangements of the greater Powers of Europe. By letters which, he said, he had received from his wife, he learned that after the Queen of Naples had returned to Vienna she had taken notice of and been very kind to his son, and that in a conversation she had with his wife she had asked her why she did not follow him (Buonaparte) to Elba. Maria Louisa answered that she wished to do so, but her father and mother would not allow her, &c.

The Queen of Naples then interrogated her as to whether she really liked him, when, being answered in the affirmative, and Maria Louisa speaking further in his favour, the queen said to her, "My child, when one has the happiness to be married to such a man, papas and mammas should not keep one away from him whilst there are windows and sheets by which an escape to him might be effected."

If there be any truth in the Archduchess having written to him in this style whilst he was at Elba, it will tend to prove that she entertained some idea of his restoration to power; for were she (as he would infer by it) really attached to him, she would, I think, have been more likely to have attempted following the Queen of Naples' advice than to have written about it.

In the course of this evening's conversation he told me that he considered the Russians and Poles to be decidedly a braver race of people than all the rest of Europe excepting the French and English, and in particular very superior to the Austrians. He said that the Emperor of Austria had neither abilities nor firmness of character; that the King of Prussia was *un pauvre bête*; that the Emperor Alexander was a more active and clever man than any of the Sovereigns of Europe, but that he was extremely false; and he asked me if I was aware that, when in friendship with him at Erfurth, he had signed with him a joint letter to the King of England to request His Majesty would relinquish the right of maritime visitation of Neutrals.

He said Russia was much to be feared if Poland was not preserved as an independent nation, to be a barrier between Russia (which was already able to call forth such hordes of soldiers) and the rest of Europe.

He added, however, that whatever might be decided on this subject at the Congress, he did not think Russia would succeed in making Poland an appendage to the Empire, the Poles being too brave and too determined ever to be brought to submit quietly to what they considered as disgrace and national degradation. He spoke in high terms of the King of Saxony, and said he was the only sovereign who had kept faith with him to the last. He mentioned to me also that, after his arrival at Paris from Elba, he had received assurances, both from the King of Spain and from the Portuguese, that, whatever appearances they might be forced to make, he might depend on their not taking any active offensive part against him. He talked to me of many of our principal characters in England, and stated particularly the high respect he entertained for the character of the late Lord Cornwallis, whose manners and behaviour at Amiens he spoke of as being most noble and honourable, both to himself and his country.

He spoke in equal terms of panegyric of Mr. Fox, with whom he said he had had much conversation when he was in France. He likewise talked of several other people in England, but not in so flattering a strain as of those I have mentioned. He told me he had formed a great friendship with Captain Usher, who conveyed him to Elba, and added that he had hoped to have seen him at Paris; that he had confidently looked for a visit from him there, and was much disappointed at his not coming to see him in his prosperity, as he had commenced acquaintance with him in his adversity.

He told me this evening, likewise, that he had gained possession of a correspondence from a foreign royal personage of high consideration in England, which spoke very disrespectfully of different branches of our Royal Family; that he (Buonaparte) had been on the point of publishing these letters in *The Moniteur*, but had desisted, or rather recalled them from the publisher, at the earnest intercession of, and from consideration towards, the person by whose means he obtained them.

Our latitude and longitude today were 40 50' N., 11 20' W.

On the 19th August, our weather was moderate with a pleasant breeze from the N.W. General Buonaparte, since on board the *Northumberland*, has kept nearly the same hours: he gets up late (between ten and eleven); he then has his breakfast (of meat and wine) in his bed-room, and continues there in his *déshabillé* until he dresses for dinner, generally between three and four in the afternoon; he then comes out of his bed cabin and either takes a short walk on deck or plays a game of chess with one of his generals until the dinner hour (which is five o'clock). At dinner he generally eats and drinks a great deal and talks but little; he prefers meats of all kinds highly dressed and never touches vegetables. After dinner he generally walks for about an hour or hour and a half, and it is during these walks that I usually have the most free and pleasant conversations with him. About eight he quits the deck, and we then make up a game at cards for him, in which he seems to engage with considerable pleasure and interest until about ten, when he retires to his bedroom, and I believe goes almost immediately to bed. Such a life of inactivity, with the quantity and description of his food, makes me fear he will not retain his health through the voyage; he however as yet does not appear to suffer any inconvenience from it.

In our conversation this evening he gave me an amusing account of being admitted a Mussulman. When in Egypt he said the *sheiks* and other chiefs there had many consultations on the subject, but at last admitted him and his followers amongst the Faithful, and with express permission to drink wine, provided that every bottle they opened they would determine to do some good action. On his requiring an explanation of what was intended by the term a good action, the head *sheik* informed him they meant such as giving charity to people in distress, making a well in a desert, building a mosque, and such like.

He said, had he continued in Egypt, things would not have ended there as they did; that Kleber was an excellent man, and a good soldier, but that he did not understand or try to manage the people of the country, and that he had beaten one of the principal *sheiks*, which, being considered an indignity to the whole, caused him to be assassinated; and he said General Menon, who succeeded him, though a brave man, had no abilities whatever. He told me the Turks had sent two or three people at different times to kill him (Buonaparte); but that the people of the country, from his having humoured them and made friends with them, always gave him sufficient warning, and prevented the assassins getting near him; whereas, he said, the man who killed Kleber had been suffered to hide himself in Kleber's garden, and when the general was walking there alone, he sprang upon him unawares and stabbed him; after which, instead of attempting to escape, he sat down at one end of the garden until he was taken by the general's guard, almost immediately after he had perpetrated the deed.

If Buonaparte had any share in causing the death of Kleber (as has been generally reported), he certainly is the most consummate hypocrite that ever existed, for I eyed him closely whilst he was talking to me about it, and he certainly did not betray the least embarrassment or hesitation whilst telling his story.

In answer to a question I put to him, he said if everything had turned out in Egypt according to the best hopes and wishes he entertained when he sailed for that country, yet, that he should nevertheless have returned as he did in consequence of the information he received from France. He played at cards as usual this evening until about half-past ten, and he appeared in excellent humour and spirits.

Our latitude and longitude this day at noon were 39 9' N. and 11 26' W.

On the 20th August the weather continued fine, and would have been pleasant but for the swell. Being Sunday, divine service was performed on board, and I was rather surprised that none of my French passengers attended, even from curiosity. I did not see the general today until dinnertime. At dinner he asked the clergyman many questions with respect to the differences between our religion and the Roman Catholic. After dinner he walked but a very short time, and then went directly to his sleeping cabin, which I attributed to his having observed the preceding Sunday that neither myself nor any of the officers of the ship joined in his card party, and his not choosing to risk infringing any of our regulations.

Our latitude and longitude today were 37 19' N. and 12 14' W.

On the 21st August our weather continued much the same, but rather more thick and cloudy, and the wind, though light, veering to the N.E. Captain Hamilton of the *Havannah*, and Captain Mansell of the 53rd, dined with me today. Buonaparte was pleasant, and talked, more than usual, with them, but on indifferent subjects. Our dinner having been later than usual, curtailed our customary walk and conversation, and he went to his card party almost immediately after getting up from dinner. He played, however, only until about half-past nine, and then retired to his bedroom. His French friends generally continue playing after he retires, until about eleven. They do not breakfast with me in the morning at eight; but have one for themselves more according to their palates, of hot meats with wines, between ten and eleven, before which time (like their chief), they seldom get up.

Our latitude and longitude today at noon were 35 56' N. and 13 16' W.

On the 22nd August we got the N.E. wind which usually prevails in these latitudes, with fine weather, though unpleasantly hazy. General Buonaparte requested me to write home from Madeira for some books for him, which I promised to do. All my French party have been engaged writing letters this day for Europe to send to Madeira as we pass it. Buonaparte asked me at dinner several questions about the different islands in the Atlantic; to what nations they belonged and so forth. His ignorance on these points seems quite wonderful, and I cannot understand what object he can have in pretending to be so if not so in reality.

He said today that had he continued at the head of the French Government in peace, and had found it to have been within his power, he never would have attempted the occupation of St. Domingo; that the most he would willingly have established with regard to that island would have been to have kept frigates and sloops stationed round it to force the blacks to receive everything they wanted from, and to export all their produce exclusively to, France; for, he added, he considered the independence of the blacks there to be more likely to prove detrimental to England than to France (and it really appears that in all his calculations he has made or does make, the proportion of evil which may accrue to England from any measure bears always in his mind the first consideration).

He complained today of suffering much from the heat: he played, however, at cards until ten o'clock and then went to his room.

Our latitude and longitude today were 34 58' N. and 13 31' W.

On the 23rd August our N.E. wind veered to E., freshened, and the weather became hot, hazy and unpleasant. Soon after noon we made the Island of Porto Santo and afterwards Madeira. General Buonaparte did not come on deck before dinner, as I expected he would have done, to look at the land, and during dinner he appeared thoughtful and out of spirits, as if the passing of this island made him reflect the more strongly on the little chance he had of ever seeing Europe again. He went upon deck, however, after dinner, and observed the island very particularly whilst we ran down along it, until we brought-to close off Funchal after dark, when he went into the cabin and played a game or two at piquet and then retired for the night to his bed-room, evidently not so well or not in such good spirits as on many of the preceding days.

We were this day at noon about nine leagues E.S.E. of Porto Santo.

On the 24th August we remained lying-to off the town of Funchal. I sent the frigate and troopships to the anchorage with my letters for England and to procure water and refreshments. We were unfortunate in having a very strong and unpleasant *siroc* wind which kept the thermometer above 80. General Buonaparte came out of his cabin earlier than usual to look at and make his remarks on the town, which he had not been able to make out last night, and he appeared better than yesterday.

Mr. Veitch, His Majesty's Consul at Madeira, came on board, and I requested him to stay dinner. Buonaparte asked him a good many questions about the island, it's produce, it's height from the level of the sea, it's population, &c. He walked with Mr. Veitch and myself, talking on general topics, for about an hour after dinner, and then retired at once to his bedroom without joining the card table.

This day at noon we were off the town of Funchal, Madeira.

On the 25th August we had a continuance of the violent and disagreeable *siroc* wind. The frigate and troopships which had anchored in Funchal Roads did not rejoin me until about three o'clock, the strength of the wind having opposed great difficulties to them in procuring their water and other supplies; and after they did join, it occupied us until dark to remove the different things they brought out for those of the squadron which had remained under way; we then made sail again to the southward.

The heat of this day and the disagreeable nature of the wind, added to the motion of the ship, which was considerable, evidently affected General Buonaparte very much. He was on deck but little either before or after dinner; he seemed to have lost his appetite, and was in very low spirits and retired early to his bedroom. We were this day at noon about seven leagues S.W. of Madeira.

On the 26th August, though the wind continued from the E. its *siroc* qualities had quitted it (to our great relief) and this proved a pleasant cool day in comparison with what we had experienced off Madeira. The sea, which had been excited by the violence of the *siroc* wind, had likewise subsided, and with scarce any motion we ran about nine knots an hour during the day. This pleasant change brought General Buonaparte out of his bedroom early, and he appeared evidently better in health, though I observed at dinner he had not recovered his former appetite.

After dinner he walked with me very late, talking generally of the affairs of Europe. He told me, amongst other things, that he had observed in some of the French papers brought from Guernsey, the King of Prussia was about to change the nature of his government, and to admit of national representation in it; he foretold that this would produce the greatest difficulties and mischief, both to the King of Prussia and Emperor of Austria; that he knew there were many revolutionary spirits in both those countries, and that the nations of the continent were not adapted for a representative government like England. I remarked to him in reply that he had, however, admitted it into the constitutions which he had himself established in France.

This he acknowledged, but added that he had not done so because he had considered it a wise measure for the nations, but because his situation at the moment required him to yield this point to the popular feeling; and it being, he said, at the time his particular interest to substantiate all the late innovations, and in short whatever differed essentially from the old system of government, thereby to render more difficult the restoration of the former order of things and therewith the dynasty of the Bourbons.

He went again over the old ground of the military bias of the French nation, and the impolicy of exasperating the French people. He spoke much of their determined aversion to the Bourbons, which he said could not but be materially increased by the idea of that family being again put in possession of the government by means of foreign troops, who had carried ruin and devastation into the greatest part of the country; therefore he was quite sure the troubles in France were by no means at an end.

They might, he said, be smothered for a moment by terror, and by the presence of the allied troops, but if these forces withdrew from the country whilst the recollection of events remained in the minds of the people, he averred that a general insurrection throughout France would immediately take place, and it would cost much difficulty and bloodshed ere it would again be suppressed.

He mentioned in the course of our conversation, that he had left his brother Jerome at Paris, who had determined to remain there in disguise for some time, and until he saw the turn affairs were likely to take; he added he did not know what befell him (Jerome) afterwards, as of course he had not been able to hear from him since.

After walking, and so conversing, in a frank strain until past nine o'clock, he went into the cabin and from thence almost immediately to his bedroom.

Our latitude and longitude this day at noon were 30 53' N., 17 22' W.

On the 27th August, we had a fine breeze from the N.E., but the weather became more than usually foggy and hazy, which I the more regretted as, General Buonaparte having expressed some curiosity respecting the Peak of Teneriffe and the Canary

Islands, I caused the squadron to be this day steered between the Islands of Gomera and Palma for the purpose of gratifying his curiosity; but though we passed close to Gomera about midday, yet the haze continued so thick that we obtained but bad views of the land, and could only make it out very imperfectly and with much difficulty.

The general seemed much recovered today; he did not, however, walk before dinner, and our days are now so much shortened by having got so far to the southward that our walks and conversations after dinner are considerably curtailed. This evening he told me he had spent 3,000,000 sterling in the improvements at Cherbourg; that he had constructed a basin, or rather a kind of inner harbour (as it is without gates), which would contain thirty sail-of-the-line and which had fifty feet of depth at low water; that the outer road, which, he said, was now perfectly safe with all winds, would also contain thirty sail-of-the-line more; that he had arranged everything necessary for building ships there, and in short for making it a naval port of the first rank; and he added that he had conceived such an establishment, so situated, would have caused us much difficulty with reference to our possessions in Guernsey and Jersey.

The only thing, he said, he had dreaded relative to it, and which he was taking therefore every precaution to avert, was our getting momentary possession of the place by a *coup de main* at any favourable juncture, and in which case he was aware that a few barrels of gunpowder, scientifically applied to the walls of his basins, cones, &c., might destroy in an instant what had cost so much time, expense, and labour to complete. He withdrew to his own cabin again very early this evening.

Today at noon we were about four leagues W. from Gomera, with a fresh breeze from the N.E., running between the Islands at the rate of about eleven miles an hour.

On the 28th August, our N.E. trade continued, but not so fresh as yesterday and the weather became hot, thermometer being from 78 to 80. My French party appeared distant and much out of humour today, especially M. de Bertrand, who presumed to appear dissatisfied because I would not desire he might be permitted to have a light burning in his cabin throughout the night. I have, of course, left them to get out of this temper their own way, and have taken little or no notice of them throughout the day. General Buonaparte took but a short walk after dinner and I had very little conversation with him.

Our latitude and longitude this day at noon were 26 2' N., 19 9' W.

On the 29th August, we had a moderate trade wind with a good deal of swell. The day has passed nearly as the preceding one with regard to my passengers, and without any circumstance worthy of notice.

Our latitude and longitude this day at noon were 24 23' N., 20 23' W.

On the 30th August, we had a fresh trade wind, disagreeable weather and heavy swell, which made the ship roll much. Buonaparte seemed to suffer much from these causes, and though he attended our dinner party he ate very little, seemed disinclined to enter into conversation, and retired to his own room again soon after dinner.

Our latitude and longitude this day at noon were 22 27' N., and 22 12' W.

On the 31st August, the fresh trade wind and swell continued; the general, however, appeared better, though the rolling of the ship seemed still to affect him considerably. He mentioned today that, when his army in Egypt was so severely visited by the plague, his soldiers, and indeed, the officers, became so disheartened that, as general-in-chief, he found it to be an absolutely necessary part of his duty to endeavour to give them confidence and reanimate them by visiting frequently himself the plague hospital, and talking to and cheering the different patients in it.

He said he caught the disorder himself but recovered again quickly; he added that those who kept up their spirits, and did not give way to the idea that they must die, generally recovered, but those who desponded almost invariably died. He played at chess with M. de Bertrand this evening till later than his usual hour of going to bed, and appeared in better spirits than for two or three days past.

Our latitude and longitude today were 19 53' N., 25 43' W.

On the 1st September, we had a fresh trade wind accompanied by uncommonly thick weather, which prevented our making out the Island of St. Antonio so soon as we expected; but, just as the sun set, we found ourselves close to the S.W. end, not having been able previously to discover any part of it. I then brought-to with an intention of communicating with the island in the morning, and to wait for two brigs I had sent to reconnoitre the nearest shores to search for a convenient watering place.

Our conversation at table this day, and afterwards on deck, was principally with reference to the islands near us, and did not draw forth anything I have considered worth noticing.

General Buonaparte has given up his evening card parties for chess, at which game he has of late entertained himself from his dinner to his bedtime.

Our latitude and longitude today at noon were 17 45' N., and 25 4' W.

On the 2nd September, about 1 a.m., the trade wind, which had been for some time strong, freshened to a perfect gale of wind, bringing with it a very heavy sea and violent rain. Soon after daylight the wind veered from N.E. to E., and then from E. to S.E. and S., still blowing hard, which rendered it impracticable for me to communicate with the islands; and the brigs I had sent to reconnoitre being driven off by the gale without effecting anything, I made the signal to put the crews of the squadron on short allowance of water, and pushed on again to the S.W. All my French passengers suffered much by the bad weather of the night; General Buonaparte, however, contrary to my expectation, made his appearance at dinner and seemed in tolerable spirits.

The weather moderated a little after dinner, and this evening passed, with regard to the general, as the preceding one, without offering anything worthy of notice.

We were today at noon W.N.W. from the S.W. end of St. Antonio, about seven leagues distance; our latitude 17 6' N.

On the 3rd September, the wind continued from the S.E. and became light, baffling and calm at times, the weather extremely hot, the thermometer being from 82 to 83 throughout the day. General Buonaparte complained much of the heat, and I saw but little of him and had no conversation with him.

I took advantage of the calm to collect returns from the squadron, and had the satisfaction to find it unusually healthy; the troopships, with 448 persons on board the one, and 446 on board the other, having the one only two, and the other only six, in their respective weekly sick reports.

Our latitude and longitude this day were 16 15' N., and 26 30' W.

On the 4th September, the calm weather which continued until a little after daylight was succeeded by a moderate breeze from the N.E., and though we had much swell from the S.W. the ship proceeded forward on her course pleasantly, which brought General Buonaparte from his cabin earlier than usual. He was occupied playing at chess before dinner, but after dinner I had a long walk and a good deal of conversation with him, in the course of which I was enabled to draw from him a relation of the Jaffa poisoning story.

His statement of it was that, finding himself obliged to evacuate Jaffa, and leave it to be taken possession of by the troops of Djezzer Pacha (whose cruelty of character was well known) he ordered off before him all the sick and wounded of the army that could be moved, to facilitate which he lent even his own horses; but the chief physician then represented to him that there were a few Frenchmen in such an advanced state of the plague that there did not remain even a possibility of their recovery, and that attempting to remove them with the rest would endanger the whole army.

Knowing, however, as he (Buonaparte) well did, that if these unhappy wretches fell into the hands of Djezzer Pacha they would have all sorts of cruelties practised on them in their last moments, he felt the best thing he could do was to order a council of all the medical men in the army to be assembled, to ascertain, in the first place, whether the removal of these poor people, or any of them, might be effected without endangering, in an unwarrantable degree, the remainder of the army, and whether there existed any chance of adequate benefit accruing to themselves if their removal were attempted; and, in the next place, if the council agreed with the chief physician and confirmed the absolute necessity of some being left behind, then to consider whether it would not be better for the individuals themselves to accelerate their death by opium rather than leave them in the state they were, to be tormented by the implacable enemies into whose hands they would inevitably be doomed to fall.

He said the council was public and everybody knew what passed in it, and therefore he had been surprised at the many contradictory stories which he knew had gone abroad respecting this transaction. He added that after the medical council had finished its deliberations, they reported to him it was their decided opinion the people ought not, on any account, to be removed, yet that the majority of the council could not bear the idea of adopting such a measure as accelerating the death of individuals under their charge, however desperate their situations; but they further stated they had every reason to believe all difficulties on this head would be done away, by the natural consequences of the disease under which these poor fellows laboured, if the general would so arrange as to retain the place forty-eight hours longer, at the expiration of which time they considered it scarcely possible that one of them could remain alive.

Upon this report, the general told me, he immediately determined on retaining Jaffa the time specified by the board, and he continued in it himself, with the whole army, twenty-four hours longer, and then left a strong rear-guard to hold it the other twenty-four hours; at the expiration of which, he said, the prediction of the medical officers was pretty well fulfilled by the death of almost every one of the patients in question, though, he added, he believed one or two might have been left not quite dead.¹ He considered the measure he wished to have adopted as more worthy of praise than of censure, and said had he been one of the people afflicted he should have considered it the greatest act of kindness to have been so dealt with, rather than left (without hope of recovery) to be tormented by such wanton savages as Djezzer Pacha's troops. Thus by his own acknowledgment (at least as far as regards his ideas and orders thereupon) is now placed beyond doubt a circumstance, which, from its nature and the numbers who have constantly denied it, has not been hitherto generally credited, and which has been also, very recently, flatly contradicted in a publication stated to have been written by a person who never quitted him for fifteen years.

In the course of this evening's conversation, Buonaparte also mentioned to me particulars of what passed between the Queen of Prussia and himself at Tilsit, when (to solicit that Magdeburg might be left to Prussia) she joined the royal party already assembled there. He said that had she arrived there sooner, it was probable she would have gained her point in this particular, not only by reason of the great advantage an extremely clever and fine woman of high rank must always have when personally urging any suit she has much at heart, but also from the inclination he (Buonaparte) then had to meet (as far as he conveniently could) the wishes of the Emperor Alexander, who he did not hesitate in affirming was at the time a strongly attached and much favoured admirer of her Prussian Majesty.

It was, he said, owing to the King of Prussia being apprised of this latter circumstance, and consequently being extremely jealous of the Emperor of Russia, that the former prevented the Queen from coming sooner to Tilsit, and until the Prussian ministers, towards the closing of the arrangements, urged him in

---

1. This part of the statement has since been confirmed to me by Captain Beattie, of the marines, serving on board the *Northumberland*, who belonged to the *Theseus* in Egypt, and entered Jaffa immediately after the French quitted it, and even before the troops of Djezzer Pacha; he assures me there were only three or four Frenchmen found alive, and those in an advanced stage of the plague.

the strongest manner to send for her, that they might have the benefit of her abilities and influence to second their endeavours to obtain better terms for Prussia; to which at length the King consenting, she arrived accordingly, and the whole party being to dine with him (General Buonaparte), she was introduced to him before dinner, and entered with great vivacity and ability upon the subject of the approaching treaty, and strongly solicited, as a personal favour to herself, that he would consent to leave Magdeburg to Prussia, which, she said, would bind her family to him by the strongest ties of gratitude, as well as respect.

The general said Her Majesty pressed her suit warmly and cleverly; but he merely replied to all she said in general terms of civility, and avoided giving her any decided answer, or entering at all with her into the merits of the question; notwithstanding, it was evident by her behaviour at dinner that she entertained sanguine hopes of succeeding. He said she sat between the Emperor of Russia and himself, and although most elegant and amiable in her manners, she did not for a moment forget the object she had in view; and in proof of this, he added that at the dessert (I think he said), or in the evening, on his offering her a rose [2] he took out of a vase near him, she, on taking it, asked him immediately if she might consider it as a token of friendship, and of his having acceded to her request. Being, however, he said, upon his guard, and resolved not to be thus caught by surprise, he parried the attack with some general remarks respecting the light in which alone civilities of this description should be regarded, and then turned the conversation.

Notwithstanding this, however, and his having been extremely cautious throughout the evening not to allow anything to escape him which might in the slightest degree authorise the queen to believe him inclined to yield to her solicitation, yet when she went away she appeared to be well satisfied, and to

---

2. I have noted particularly what the general told me respecting this rose, and his conversation at the time with the Queen of Prussia, as the author of the book "stated to be written by a person who never quitted him for fifteen years" mentions this circumstance, but states it very differently.

have persuaded herself that her endeavours were not to prove unsuccessful. The general said that therefore, thinking it would be impolitic to leave the question any longer open to discussion, he caused the Treaty to be signed at once on the next morning, and, of course, without any alterations in it in favour of Prussia.

When the queen came the next day to dinner, he said she showed evidently by her manner that she was piqued and much hurt, but she behaved with great dignity, and did not once allude to the Treaty, nor to anything which had passed respecting it, until going away in the evening, when, as General Buonaparte was handing her to her carriage, she mentioned to him how much he had disappointed her by the refusal of her request: that, had he complied, it would have attached her whole family to him forever, and so forth; to which he only answered that he should ever consider it one of the greatest misfortunes of his life that it had not been within his power to obey Her Majesty's commands in this affair, begging her, however, to believe it would always afford him the highest gratification to be able to meet any wish of hers, and adding more civil speeches of this kind; ("*mais*" said he to me, with a self-applauding smile, "*tout cela n'etoit pas Magdebourg*,") and having reached her carriage he put her into it, bade her good night, and left her.

He added that previous, however, to her driving off, she sent for Duroc (the Grand Maréchal of his palace) to her carriage, when, giving vent to her feelings, which she had till then so well stifled, she could not refrain from tears whilst she complained to him of the great disappointment, and told him how much she had been deceived in Buonaparte's character, and hurt by what had passed, &c., and early the next morning he said he received a message from her to say that, being taken suddenly ill, she had been forced to quit Tilsit and return home; and thus, he added, Magdeburg was retained, though perhaps he had suffered somewhat by it in the good graces of her Prussian Majesty. He told me he thought her a most elegant engaging woman, and as handsome as could be expected in a woman thirty-five years of age. He spoke, however, very badly of her character as a wife, and particularly with reference to the Emperor Alexander; to oblige whom, he mentioned (as a good joke), that he detained the King of Prussia a whole day by announcing an intention of paying him a formal visit, of which the Emperor Alexander took a premeditated advantage by setting off to obtain thereby an uninterrupted *tête-à-tête* visit with the queen!!!

Having walked with me recounting these stories till later than usual, he did not make his appearance in the great cabin but retired to his own room at once.

Our latitude and longitude this day at noon were 15 34' N. and 26 36' W.

On the 5th September we had a moderate trade wind but excessively hot weather, and nothing occurred during the day with regard to General Buonaparte worthy of notice. Our latitude and longitude at noon was 13 58' N. and 25 30' W.

On the 6th September our trade wind continued till about four in the evening, when we experienced excessively heavy rain, and the wind gradually died away until it failed us altogether and was succeeded by a southerly wind. To my great surprise, after General Buonaparte had eaten his dinner he got up to take his walk as usual, and upon my remarking to him that it was still pouring with rain, and therefore advising him not to go out in it, he treated it lightly and said it would not hurt him more than the sailors he observed at the time catching water, working and running about in it. Of course I no longer opposed his whim, and out he went in the rain accompanied by two of his French friends, who, though obliged to attend him, seemed by no means to enjoy the idea of the wetting they were doomed to get *par complaisance*.

I have no doubt General Buonaparte intended this dash of his should give us a great idea of his hardiness of character; as, however, no further particular notice was taken of it by any of us, and finding it, I suppose, more unpleasant than he expected, his walk was of very short duration, and being, as was inevitable, perfectly wet through, he, immediately on quitting the deck, went into his own cabin, from whence he did not rejoin us during the evening.

Our latitude and longitude this day at noon were 12 41' N. and 23 55' W.

From the 6th to this day, the 23rd September (on which we crossed the Equator about the meridian of Greenwich), General Buonaparte, continuing to keep nearly the same hours, and to follow the same routine of eating, drinking and sleeping, as before noticed, and my usual conversations with him after dinner having suffered considerable interruption from the shortness of the evenings and from his own people keeping more closely about him during his evening walks than formerly, so little variety of matter has offered for detailing on each successive day that I have been induced to combine this period; throughout the most of which we have experienced moderate S.S.W. winds with cloudy weather, accompanied occasionally with rain, and the air from these causes has been more cool and pleasant than we expected to meet with in such latitudes.

In the course of the different short conversations I managed to have with the general in this interval, he told me that had he succeeded in his attempt against England and reached London, his chief object and first endeavour would have been to have there concluded a peace, which he should have immediately offered on moderate terms; but what, under such circumstances, he would have considered moderate terms I could not draw from him (nor did I think it very material), but the relinquishment of the right of maritime visitation of neutrality was one of the points he certainly would have insisted upon. In another conversation on the subject of the Russian expedition, he assured me in the strongest manner that the only object he had when he undertook it, and all he should have asked had he been successful, was the independence of Poland (to which nation he intended leaving the free choice of their own king, only recommending Poniatowsky to them as worthy of such distinction), and to make the Emperor of Russia engage to join firmly in the continental system against commercial intercourse of any sort with England until its Government should be brought to agree to what he termed "the Independence of the Seas."

He, however, when subsequently talking to me of Moscow, let out that he had procured there numerous emissaries to disperse throughout the country amongst the Russian peasantry to bias them in his favour and against their own Government; to explain to them the miseries they suffered from the unjust state of slavery in which they were kept; and to offer them freedom and protection if they would seek it through his means. He said he had at the time already received applications from different bodies of them, and had he been able to have maintained himself in the country he was quite sure he should have had the mass of the population in his favour. He told me that, prior to the death of the Emperor Paul, he (Buonaparte), whilst he was First Consul, had received seven or eight letters, written in His Imperial Majesty's own hand, pressing him to enter into close and intimate alliance with Russia, for the express purpose of exerting the united efforts of the two countries to humble Great Britain; and the Emperor proposed (if Buonaparte approved of it) to send off at once a large Russian army to act against the English interests in India.

The general said he was about to dispatch a confidential ambassador with full powers to make the necessary arrangements, and to communicate to the Emperor his sentiments on these points, when he received the unwelcome intelligence of the Emperor's assassination. He added that, from the opinion the Emperor Paul seemed by his letters to entertain of him (the general), and from the great confidence he appeared to place in him, he had no doubt, if their negotiation had gone on, he would shortly have attained sufficient ascendancy with the Emperor to have induced him to change the foolish and impolitic course he was then pursuing in his own country; in which case his life would probably have been saved, and he might have become an ally of great importance to the French, and therefore the general said he considered Paul's death at the moment as a particularly untoward circumstance.

In a conversation on the propriety of the different capitals of Europe being sufficiently fortified to enable them to withstand for a short time a sudden advance and attack of an enemy's army, he told me he had long foreseen the propriety of having works of this kind around Paris, but he had been restrained from ordering them by his dread of the effect it might have on the public opinion, in concert with which he had considered it a requisite policy always to act, and which, even in the zenith of his power, he had never felt himself strong enough to disregard; and, he added, he knew full well the French character to be such that until danger was at their gates they could not have borne the idea of such a precaution being for a moment necessary.

Speaking again on the subject of his meditated invasion of England, I asked him if he had procured any plans of our fortifications at Chatham. He told me he had not, but that he had a general idea of the lines there, and that he had had no doubt of procuring in time such further information on the subject as was necessary for him. He said he had got his intelligence very regularly from England by means of our smuggling boats, and that amongst others Mr. Goldsmith (the Editor) had conveyed to him much useful information. He told me he had had a personal interview with him at Boulogne at one of the periods he (Goldsmith) came over in one of these smuggling boats, and he said considerable sums had been paid him by the police office at different times for services of this nature.

I mention this because I have determined to note down herein every particular this extraordinary man tells; but it is right I should at the same time remark that there was a something of malicious cunning in General Buonaparte's manner whilst making this statement which induced me very much to doubt the truth of the whole story; and I was rather inclined to think he made this assertion (which was in public, at my table) either with a view to make us fancy all Mr. Goldsmith had written against him was merely as a cloak to cover his (Goldsmith's) own treasons, or (which is perhaps more probable) he hoped by such a statement so made, and therefore likely to be repeated, that he might cause public suspicion to fall on Mr. Goldsmith, which might perhaps draw him into difficulties, and thereby offer General Buonaparte some chance of being revenged upon him for the unqualified abuse he has so lavishly heaped upon the general and his family. He further observed that he believed Mr. Goldsmith was possessed of some talent, although a consummate rogue, and he then immediately turned the conversation to other matter.

On another day, talking of Ireland, he told me he had arranged everything with that country, and if he could have got safely over to it the force he intended sending, the party there in his favour was so strong that he had every reason to suppose they would have succeeded in possessing themselves of the whole island. He said he had held constant communication with the disaffected party, which he averred was by no means confined to the Roman Catholics, but had also a very large proportion of Protestants. He of course did not give me any of their names, nor did I think it right to ask him for them. He said he always acquiesced in everything they asked for, leaving all arrangements respecting the country, religion, &c., entirely to themselves; his grand and only object being to gain the advantageous point, for him, of separating Ireland from England on any terms, and to have it on his side in opposition to England.

He told me those who came to him from Ireland generally came and returned through London, by which means he obtained information from them respecting both countries; and they crossed the Channel backwards and forwards with little risk or difficulty by the means likewise of his friends the smugglers; but he said, notwithstanding the great advantages he thus derived from these smugglers, he found out at last that they played a similar game backwards and forwards, and carried us as much intelligence to England as they brought him from it, and he was therefore obliged to forbid their being any longer admitted at Dunkirk, or indeed anywhere but at Gravelines; where he established particular regulations respecting them, and did not allow them to pass a barrier which he caused to be fixed for the purpose, and where he placed a guard to watch them, and to prevent their having unnecessary communication with the country; and he ordered the goods and other articles they wished to have to be brought down for them to this barrier, for which they paid a small additional impost.

Soon after we had crossed the Equator today, the Comte de Bertrand came to me from

General Buonaparte to say that, it being a general custom of all nations for those who had not passed the Equator to submit to certain ceremonies, or to pay for exemption some trifling tribute to those who had crossed it, he (the general) wished, if I had no objection to it, to send our seamen, who were at the time going through the usual process, one or two hundred *napoleons*. As I considered this to be an attempt of the general's to avail himself, with his usual finesse, of a plausible excuse to distribute such a large sum amongst the seamen, solely with a view of rendering himself popular with them, I, of course, not only refused my assent to this request, but pointedly prohibited it. I told him the custom of the ships of our nation was, for those whose rank and station authorized them to look for indulgence on these occasions, usually to send a bottle of rum to the seamen; but this being incompatible with the discipline of a man-of-war, officers of the *Northumberland* who had not crossed the line, had given, in lieu of rum, the subordinate officers one dollar, and the higher officers half-a-guinea each, and if General Buonaparte felt extremely anxious to give something more, I would, though reluctantly, say he might give as far as five *napoleons*; but that that sum was the utmost I could allow of under existing circumstances.

The Grand Maréchal, in reply, endeavoured to persuade me that what General Buonaparte should give on such an occasion ought not to be weighed by what was given by officers of the profession, and that the sum of one hundred *napoleons* was the least which such a person could offer on so extraordinary an occasion as his crossing the Equator. His rhetoric, however, as usual, not having the slightest effect towards changing my determination, he was forced to return back to his master with my answer, who very wisely let the matter then drop, and did not say anything further on the subject, nor did he by his manner at dinner show that he was hurt or piqued by the refusal. I understand, however, he did not send the five *napoleons* for which I granted permission.

It is worthy of remark that this day we have passed zero of latitude and zero of longitude, and the sun the zero of its declination.

From the 23rd September to this day, the 6th October (which period, like the preceding, I combine to avoid uninteresting monotonous details), we have had the wind with little or no variation from S.W., accompanied with a heavy swell from the westward, the weather being cloudy and very cool, almost indeed amounting to cold, but without rain. By continuing pertinaciously on the starboard tack for the purpose of gaining all the southing possible, in the hope of thereby meeting sooner the S.E. trade-wind, we have got as near as within thirty leagues of the coast, in latitude 9 36', but the wind having today veered somewhat more to the southward has at last enabled me to put the ship's head to the westward with some prospect of advantage, and gives me reason to hope our distance from St. Helena will now be quickly diminished, which indeed is not less anxiously desired by myself than by my passengers, as restless Frenchmen with a foul wind make but unpleasant messmates. They have, however, continued better in health than could be reasonably expected considering the changes of climate they have gone through, the length of time since their first embarkation in the *Bellerophon*, and the inactive life they have led in comparison with that to which they have been accustomed.

Of the whole party Madame de Bertrand only has experienced a few days' confinement from a feverish attack, which, however, yielded almost immediately to bleeding, and amongst all the rest there has not been a complaint beyond a cold or sore throat of trifling nature and short continuance. General Buonaparte himself is certainly fatter and looking better than when he first came on board the *Northumberland*, and I must say he has throughout shown far less impatience about the wind or the weather, and made less difficulties, than any of the rest of the party. Subsequently to the 23rd *ultimo*, in our conversations, he has mentioned to me that he caused, a short time back, a survey to be taken throughout France of the grown oak timber it contained fit for ship building, the report made to him upon which stated that there was actually sufficient quantity for building a thousand sail of the line; but, he said, France failed altogether in trees fit for masts, and those they were therefore obliged to get from the Baltic; but he having understood that the Corsican firs were strong and tough enough to serve for masts during the two years immediately after they were cut down (after which only they lost their elasticity and became brittle), and as nine of them could be brought to France at as little expense as one from the Baltic, he had latterly endeavoured to bring the Corsican spars into use in the French navy, authorising their being sawn up for plank or other use after having served as topmasts for two years.

But this plan, he said, did not appear to be much approved of by the people of the Marine Department, as there existed extraordinary prejudice throughout the French navy against masts made from any spars except those brought from the Baltic. He told me there was a large quantity of masts belonging to the French Government at Copenhagen when Lord Nelson made the attack and consequent convention there; that he (the general) had been therefore, at the time, alarmed for the safety of his spars, but the Danes kept their faith with him and he afterwards got them all safe to France. Some of them, he said, he was obliged to have brought almost the whole way by inland navigation, being much in want of them, and the coast being too closely watched by our cruisers to allow of his trusting them round by sea.

Speaking of the present navy of France, he told me some of the superior officers were tolerably good seamen, he believed, but none of them were good officers; that the best of them had been taken during the Revolution from the India and other merchant service, and, the French navy having been so little employed, they were quite unaccustomed to command in any very difficult or trying circumstances; therefore, that when they had accidentally fallen into such situations, they always appeared to have lost their heads, and become quite confused, and that whatever they did was generally precisely what they ought not. He said Admiral Gantheaume did very well while with him (the general) at his elbow when they were coming from Egypt; but, he added, if Admiral Gantheaume had been left to himself he would have been taken twenty times over, for he was constantly wanting to change the ship's course to avoid one enemy or another, and would have, by such over-precautions, lost as much by night as he gained by day.

He therefore, he said, obliged the admiral always to explain to him upon paper the exact situation of the ship and the apprehended danger, after which it almost always occurred that he took upon himself to desire the admiral to continue on a straight course for Fréjus; and to this alone he attributed their having got safe in, as the admiral's anxiety would certainly have induced him to have acted very differently had not he (the general) so interfered with him, and thus left it to the admiral only to exert his seamanship to press the ships forward. He told me also it was a curious fact that Admiral Bruix, on their way up to Alexandria, had actually explained to him very minutely the decided disadvantage a fleet must labour under by receiving at anchor an attack from an hostile fleet under sail; and yet, from want of recollection and presence of mind upon emergencies, which the general had alluded to, this admiral, a few weeks afterwards, received at anchor Lord Nelson's attack, losing his own life and nearly his whole fleet to exemplify the correctness of his ideas and the impropriety of his conduct; but which General Buonaparte said he was positive would not have happened (at least inasmuch as relates to the fighting at anchor) had he, the general, been on the spot.

He added, on the same subject, that it struck him the French admirals had generally, upon coming to action, lost too much time and been too anxious about forming lines and making manoeuvres which had ultimately proved of no adequate advantage; he had therefore desired they might be instructed that, for the future, on approaching an enemy, a signal to form a line, as convenient for mutual support, and afterwards a signal to engage, would always be deemed fully sufficient to make to those under their orders; and after this the captain of every ship of the fleet was to be held individually responsible to the Government for getting the ship he commanded quickly into close battle, and doing his best towards the destruction of some one of the enemy; which would at all events prevent the captains from covering their own neglect (as Dumanois had done) by attributing errors to their chief.

He had, however, he said, latterly resolved (unless some extraordinary emergency made it necessary) not to venture any more line-of-battle ships to sea until he should have had it in his power to have sent from his different ports at once 120 sail of the line, for the making up of which number, he said, he had laid all his plans; and he affirmed that, from the efforts he intended to have made for the object, he believed very much time would not have elapsed before he would have completed them.

In the meantime, he said, whatever it might have cost him, he had determined on always keeping ten sail of French frigates at sea for the purpose of making and improving his officers. He added that when his frigates had been sent on distant cruises they were apt to consider their danger pretty well over when once safely through our line of cruisers on the French coast, after which they generally relaxed their vigilance and precautions. He had, therefore, decided to order these ten frigates for the future to cruise only in the neighbourhood of England or Ireland, where they would be certain to have enemies, bad weather and dangerous coasts, to keep them always on the alert; and those who managed to escape being wrecked or captured must, of course, do much more mischief to our commerce than had ever been done by the French frigates heretofore sent into the open seas and southern latitudes!

To the commanders of all those, he said, who returned safe

from such service, he should have given great promotion and rewards, and as fast as he heard of any being taken or lost he should have supplied their places with fresh ones. On my remarking to him the difficulty I conceived he would have found in obtaining seamen to have followed up this plan, he told me, by the system of conscription for the marine, which he had lately established in all the maritime counties of France, he would have had as many seamen as he pleased. Its customary production, without any vexation, would have given him 20,000 men a year; and, he added that, already, for want of ships to put these seamen in, he had been obliged to form them into regiments for the protection of the coast. (These men, however, it must be observed herefrom, would only have been seamen because he chose to have them designated as such; not from any claim of having been to sea or of having served on shipboard, but merely because they had been born and raised in a maritime county).

In a conversation respecting the late campaigns, he told me that at the Battle of Wagram he had had under his command, actually engaged in the field, a greater number of men than in any of his other battles; they amounted, he said, to about 180,000, and that he had had at the same time in the field 1,000 pieces of cannon. At Moscow, he said, though not much short of the same number, yet he certainly had not quite so many; and at Leipsic he did not think that he had more than 140,000. In answer to a question I put to him, he told me he considered a General Clausel to be decidedly the most able military officer now in France. Maréchal Soult and others of the *maréchals* were, he said, brave and able men for carrying into execution operations previously planned; but to plan and execute with large armies, in his opinion, none of them were by any means equal to this General Clausel.

The troopships having fallen considerably to leeward today, I have determined not to wait any longer for them; being now so far on the voyage they must, at all events, get to St Helena a day or two after me.

From the 6th October the wind, remaining from S.S.W. to

S., allowed us to continue on the larboard tack without losing ground to the northward, until we got at last the S.E. Trade on the 11th inst., having, however, previously passed the thirteenth degree S. latitude; and even then the Trade hung considerably to the southward, but the ship being so much to windward this became immaterial to us, and with a fine, strong, fair wind we made between two and three hundred miles a day until we reached St. Helena this morning (the 15th), the sixty-sixth day since we quitted the Lizard. During the latter part of the voyage, General Buonaparte, speaking to me of himself, told me that it was the want of officers at the beginning of the Revolutionary War which caused him to be sent for (though then a very young captain of artillery) from the Northern Frontier, where he was serving, to take the command of the artillery before Toulon; that almost immediately after his arrival at this station he had pointed out to General Corteaux the necessity of making a great effort to get possession of the place which was called Fort Mulgrave by us, which Buonaparte engaged to succeed in doing if General Corteaux would allow him, and foretold that that place, once taken, would oblige the English, immediately afterwards, to entirely evacuate Toulon.

This proposal, however, General Corteaux would not listen to, and they therefore went on some time longer according to their former plans of attack without materially advancing in the siege or doing any real good, until, one of the Representatives of the People coming to the army to overlook what they were about (as was customary in those days), Buonaparte directly laid before him his plans, and, obtaining his approval, Corteaux was overruled and obliged to adopt the measures which Buonaparte had before proposed to him; which succeeding precisely according to his prediction, he was in reward immediately promoted to the rank of general of brigade.

He afterwards went with part of the same army into Savoy, where he rendered some further services; but it having been just then determined, in consequence of a scarcity of officers for the infantry, to draft into it some of the officers of the artillery, and it falling to his (General Buonaparte's) lot to be one of these, he quitted the army and went to Paris to remonstrate, and to endeavour to avoid being so exchanged; but meeting with an unfavourable reception from a general of artillery, who was a representative of the people and had the chief management of these arrangements.

After some high words passing between them he (Buonaparte) retired in disgust, and putting on the dress of the Institute of Paris, to which he then belonged (having been elected into it in consequence of his proficiency in mathematics), he continued in Paris endeavouring to keep quiet and from the armies; which, he said, however, he should have been obliged to have joined (perhaps in a subordinate capacity), had not the advance of the Austrian General, De Vins, into Italy, and the retreat and alarm of the French army opposed to him, spread considerable consternation in Paris; which induced the Committee of Public Safety (that knew General Buonaparte was well acquainted with the geography of that country) to send for him to consult with him on the best measures to be adopted; and they were so satisfied with what he laid before them on the subject that they immediately caused him to draw up instructions for their general in Italy founded upon his (Buonaparte's) advice; and the Committee then directed that General Buonaparte might remain near them at Paris to assist them on such military points as they might wish to consult him upon.

The advice he gave, as above mentioned, proved efficacious; their Italian army took up the position he had pointed out, and thereby was enabled to stand its ground without falling any further back, in spite of every effort of the Austrian general to force it, until it became strong enough to attack in its turn; which it ultimately did, and then (as is well known) defeated De Vins, and was completely successful. Considerable credit accrued to General Buonaparte on this account, and he remained at Paris attached to the Committee of Public Safety until the 13th *Vendemaire*, the day on which the Convention was attacked by the revolted sections of Paris; which last having gained considerable advantages over the troops of the Convention, then under the command of General Menon, Buonaparte was sent for by the Convention and placed in command of the troops, in lieu of General Menon; and he (Buonaparte) soon succeeding in defeating the people of the section and in restoring order, was as a reward immediately made Commandant of Paris; which situation, he said, gave him considerable consequence and in which he continued until he was made commander-in-chief of the Army of Italy.

But he told me it was not until the Battle of Lodi that any idea of his rising sufficiently in consequence to authorise his someday interfering in the Government of France, entered his imagination; but then, finding all his plans succeed so beyond even his own expectations, he began to look forward, though without any decided plan, to such events as afterwards took place; and he said the quantity of money which he sent from Italy to France, with these views, increased very considerably his popularity; but after his campaign of Italy and the consequent suspension of hostilities with Austria.

He said the Directory became very jealous of him and were therefore anxious to get him into a scrape, to avoid which required his utmost caution and *finesse*, and induced him to refuse an appointment which had been offered to him to conduct the diplomatic discussions then going on with Austria, as also soon afterwards an appointment offered to him to command an army for the invasion of England; but when the command of an expedition to Egypt was proposed to him, he immediately saw the advantage it offered him for getting out of the way of a jealous arbitrary Government, by its measures running itself to ruin, and by placing him at the head of an army for an expedition almost certain to be successful, leaving it open to him to return with increased popularity whenever he might judge the crisis favourable; therefore, he said, the Directory being anxious to get him out of France and he being equally anxious to get away from them, the Egyptian Expedition did not fail to please both parties, and he warmly entered into it the moment it was proposed;

but he assured me that the proposition did not originate with himself, as has been generally supposed

He said, having left France with these ideas, he was anxiously looking for the events which brought him back even before they happened; and on his return to France he was soon well assured that there no longer existed in it a party strong enough to oppose him. He, therefore, immediately planned the Revolution of the 18th *Brumaire*, and though he might, he said, on that day have run some little personal risk owing to the general confusion, yet everything was so arranged that it could not possibly have failed, and the Government of France from that day became inevitably and irretrievably in his hands and those of his adherents; and therefore, he said, all the stories I might have heard of intentions of arresting him about that time, and of opposing his intentions, were all nonsense and without foundation in truth, for his plans had been too long and too well laid to admit of being so counteracted.

After he became First Consul he said plots and conspiracies against his life had, however, been very frequent, but by vigilance and some good fortune they had all been discovered and frustrated. He told me the one nearest proving fatal to him was that in which Pichegru and Georges (and, he added, Moreau) were concerned. He said thirty-six of this party had been actually in Paris six weeks, without the police knowing anything of it; which was at last discovered by means of an emigrant apothecary who, being informed against and secured after landing from an English man-of-war (and the police having entertained some suspicions in consequence of the numbers that had been reported to have been clandestinely landed about the same time), it was judged would be a likely person to bring to confession if properly managed; therefore, being condemned to death and every preparation made for his execution, his life was offered him if he could give any intelligence sufficiently important to merit such indulgence; when he immediately caught at the offer and gave the names of the thirty-six persons before mentioned, every one of whom, with Pichegru and Georges, were (by the vigorous measures immediately adopted) found and secured in Paris within a fortnight.

He said that, previous to this plot being discovered, it would probably have proved fatal to him, had not Georges insisted upon being appointed a consul, which Moreau and Pichegru would not hear of, and therefore Georges and his party could not be brought to act. He told me also that it was to be at hand for the purpose of aiding in these conspiracies, and to take advantage of any confusion they might create, that the Duc D'Enghien took up his residence in the neighbourhood of Strasburg, in which town he (Buonaparte) maintained that he had certain information of the duke having been in disguise several times.

On my asking him if a report I had heard was true of his having sent an order for the duke's reprieve, but which, unfortunately, arrived too late, he told me it certainly was not true; that the duke was condemned for having conspired against France, and he (Buonaparte) was determined from the first to let the law take its course respecting him, to endeavour if possible to check these frequent conspiracies. And in answer to my remonstrating against his having taken the duke from the territories of the Duke of Baden, he said this did not, in his opinion, at all alter the case between France and the Duc D'Enghien; that the Duke of Baden might certainly have had some reason to complain of the violation of his territory, but that was an affair for him to settle with the Duke of Baden and not with the Duc D'Enghien; whom when they had got within the territory of France (no matter how), they had full right to try and punish for any act against the existing Government committed by him in France.

Thus does this man reason, who now exclaims so violently against the legality of our conduct in refusing to receive him in England, and sending him to reside at St. Helena.

22nd October. Since General Buonaparte's arrival at St. Helena I have been so occupied that I have seen but little of him. I went with him, however, one day to Longwood, and he seemed tolerably satisfied with it, though with his attendants he has since been complaining a good deal; and having stated to me that he could not bear the crowds which gathered to see him in the town, he has, at his own request, been permitted to take up his residence (until Longwood should be completed) at a small house called the Briars, where there is a pretty good garden, and a tolerably large room, detached from the house, of which he has taken possession, and in which and the garden he remains almost all day; but in the evenings I understand he has regularly invited himself to join the family party in the house, where he plays at whist with the ladies of the family for sugar-plums until his usual hour of retiring for the night.

ALSO FROM LEONAUR
AVAILABLE IN SOFTCOVER OR HARDCOVER WITH DUST JACKET

CAPTAIN OF THE 95th (Rifles) *by Jonathan Leach*—An officer of Wellington's Sharpshooters during the Peninsular, South of France and Waterloo Campaigns of the Napoleonic Wars.

BUGLER AND OFFICER OF THE RIFLES *by William Green & Harry Smith* With the 95th (Rifles) during the Peninsular & Waterloo Campaigns of the Napoleonic Wars

BAYONETS, BUGLES AND BONNETS *by James 'Thomas' Todd*—Experiences of hard soldiering with the 71st Foot - the Highland Light Infantry - through many battles of the Napoleonic wars including the Peninsular & Waterloo Campaigns

THE ADVENTURES OF A LIGHT DRAGOON *by George Farmer & G.R. Gleig*—A cavalryman during the Peninsular & Waterloo Campaigns, in captivity & at the siege of Bhurtpore, India

THE COMPLEAT RIFLEMAN HARRIS *by Benjamin Harris as told to & transcribed by Captain Henry Curling*—The adventures of a soldier of the 95th (Rifles) during the Peninsular Campaign of the Napoleonic Wars

WITH WELLINGTON'S LIGHT CAVALRY *by William Tomkinson*—The Experiences of an officer of the 16th Light Dragoons in the Peninsular and Waterloo campaigns of the Napoleonic Wars.

SURTEES OF THE RIFLES *by William Surtees*—A Soldier of the 95th (Rifles) in the Peninsular campaign of the Napoleonic Wars.

ENSIGN BELL IN THE PENINSULAR WAR *by George Bell*—The Experiences of a young British Soldier of the 34th Regiment 'The Cumberland Gentlemen' in the Napoleonic wars.

WITH THE LIGHT DIVISION *by John H. Cooke*—The Experiences of an Officer of the 43rd Light Infantry in the Peninsula and South of France During the Napoleonic Wars

NAPOLEON'S IMPERIAL GUARD: FROM MARENGO TO WATERLOO *by J. T. Headley*—This is the story of Napoleon's Imperial Guard from the bearskin caps of the grenadiers to the flamboyance of their mounted chasseurs, their principal characters and the men who commanded them.

BATTLES & SIEGES OF THE PENINSULAR WAR *by W. H. Fitchett*—Corunna, Busaco, Albuera, Ciudad Rodrigo, Badajos, Salamanca, San Sebastian & Others

AVAILABLE ONLINE AT **www.leonaur.com**
AND OTHER GOOD BOOK STORES

ALSO FROM LEONAUR
AVAILABLE IN SOFTCOVER OR HARDCOVER WITH DUST JACKET

WELLINGTON AND THE PYRENEES CAMPAIGN VOLUME I: FROM VITORIA TO THE BIDASSOA by *F. C. Beatson*—The final phase of the campaign in the Iberian Peninsula.

WELLINGTON AND THE INVASION OF FRANCE VOLUME II: THE BIDASSOA TO THE BATTLE OF THE NIVELLE by *F. C. Beatson*—The second of Beatson's series on the fall of Revolutionary France published by Leonaur, the reader is once again taken into the centre of Wellington's strategic and tactical genius.

WELLINGTON AND THE FALL OF FRANCE VOLUME III: THE GAVES AND THE BATTLE OF ORTHEZ by *F. C. Beatson*—This final chapter of F. C. Beatson's brilliant trilogy shows the 'captain of the age' at his most inspired and makes all three books essential additions to any Peninsular War library.

NAVAL BATTLES OF THE NAPOLEONIC WARS by *W. H. Fitchett*—Cape St. Vincent, the Nile, Cadiz, Copenhagen, Trafalgar & Others

SERGEANT GUILLEMARD: THE MAN WHO SHOT NELSON? by *Robert Guillemard*—A Soldier of the Infantry of the French Army of Napoleon on Campaign Throughout Europe

WITH THE GUARDS ACROSS THE PYRENEES by *Robert Batty*—The Experiences of a British Officer of Wellington's Army During the Battles for the Fall of Napoleonic France, 1813.

A STAFF OFFICER IN THE PENINSULA by *E. W. Buckham*—An Officer of the British Staff Corps Cavalry During the Peninsula Campaign of the Napoleonic Wars

THE LEIPZIG CAMPAIGN: 1813—NAPOLEON AND THE "BATTLE OF THE NATIONS" by *F. N. Maude*—Colonel Maude's analysis of Napoleon's campaign of 1813.

BUGEAUD: A PACK WITH A BATON by *Thomas Robert Bugeaud*—The Early Campaigns of a Soldier of Napoleon's Army Who Would Become a Marshal of France.

TWO LEONAUR ORIGINALS

SERGEANT NICOL by *Daniel Nicol*—The Experiences of a Gordon Highlander During the Napoleonic Wars in Egypt, the Peninsula and France.

WATERLOO RECOLLECTIONS by *Frederick Llewellyn*—Rare First Hand Accounts, Letters, Reports and Retellings from the Campaign of 1815.

AVAILABLE ONLINE AT **www.leonaur.com**
AND OTHER GOOD BOOK STORES

ALSO FROM LEONAUR
AVAILABLE IN SOFTCOVER OR HARDCOVER WITH DUST JACKET

THE JENA CAMPAIGN: 1806 by *F. N. Maude*—The Twin Battles of Jena & Auerstadt Between Napoleon's French and the Prussian Army.

PRIVATE O'NEIL by *Charles O'Neil*—The recollections of an Irish Rogue of H. M. 28th Regt.—The Slashers— during the Peninsula & Waterloo campaigns of the Napoleonic wars.

ROYAL HIGHLANDER by *James Anton*—A soldier of H.M 42nd (Royal) Highlanders during the Peninsular, South of France & Waterloo Campaigns of the Napoleonic Wars.

CAPTAIN BLAZE by *Elzéar Blaze*—Elzéar Blaze recounts his life and experiences in Napoleon's army in a well written, articulate and companionable style.

LEJEUNE VOLUME 1 by *Louis-François Lejeune*—The Napoleonic Wars through the Experiences of an Officer on Berthier's Staff.

LEJEUNE VOLUME 2 by *Louis-François Lejeune*—The Napoleonic Wars through the Experiences of an Officer on Berthier's Staff.

FUSILIER COOPER by *John S. Cooper*—Experiences in the 7th (Royal) Fusiliers During the Peninsular Campaign of the Napoleonic Wars and the American Campaign to New Orleans.

CAPTAIN COIGNET by *Jean-Roch Coignet*—A Soldier of Napoleon's Imperial Guard from the Italian Campaign to Russia and Waterloo.

FIGHTING NAPOLEON'S EMPIRE by *Joseph Anderson*—The Campaigns of a British Infantryman in Italy, Egypt, the Peninsular & the West Indies During the Napoleonic Wars.

CHASSEUR BARRES by *Jean-Baptiste Barres*—The experiences of a French Infantryman of the Imperial Guard at Austerlitz, Jena, Eylau, Friedland, in the Peninsular, Lutzen, Bautzen, Zinnwald and Hanau during the Napoleonic Wars.

MARINES TO 95TH (RIFLES) by *Thomas Fernyhough*—The military experiences of Robert Fernyhough during the Napoleonic Wars.

HUSSAR ROCCA by *Albert Jean Michel de Rocca*—A French cavalry officer's experiences of the Napoleonic Wars and his views on the Peninsular Campaigns against the Spanish, British And Guerilla Armies.

SERGEANT BOURGOGNE by *Adrien Bourgogne*—With Napoleon's Imperial Guard in the Russian Campaign and on the Retreat from Moscow 1812 - 13.

AVAILABLE ONLINE AT **www.leonaur.com**
AND OTHER GOOD BOOK STORES

www.ingramcontent.com/pod-product-compliance
Lightning Source LLC
Chambersburg PA
CBHW021010090426
42738CB00007B/735